The Idols of ISIS

THE IDOLS OF ISIS

FROM ASSYRIA TO THE INTERNET

Aaron Tugendhaft

The University of Chicago Press
Chicago and London

The University of Chicago Press, Chicago 60637
The University of Chicago Press, Ltd., London

Published 2020

29 28 27 26 25 24 23 22 21 20   1 2 3 4 5

ISBN-13: 978-0-226-62353-5 (cloth)
ISBN-13: 978-0-226-73756-0 (paper)
ISBN-13: 978-0-226-62367-2 (e-book)
DOI: https://doi.org/10.7208/chicago/9780226623672.001.0001

Library of Congress Cataloging-in-Publication Data

Names: Tugendhaft, Aaron, author.
Title: The idols of ISIS : from Assyria to the internet / Aaron Tugendhaft.
Description: Chicago : University of Chicago Press, 2020. | Includes bibliographical references.
Identifiers: LCCN 2020007574 | ISBN 9780226623535 (cloth) | ISBN 9780226737560 (paperback) | ISBN 9780226623672 (ebook)
Subjects: LCSH: Matḥaf al-Mawṣil. | IS (Organization) | Iconoclasm—Middle East. | Cultural property—Destruction and pillage—Middle East. | Idols and images—Middle East. | Motion pictures in propaganda. | Mass media and propaganda. | Islamic fundamentalism—Middle East.
Classification: LCC N9103 .T84 2020 | DDC 700/.4820218—dc23
LC record available at https://lccn.loc.gov/2020007574

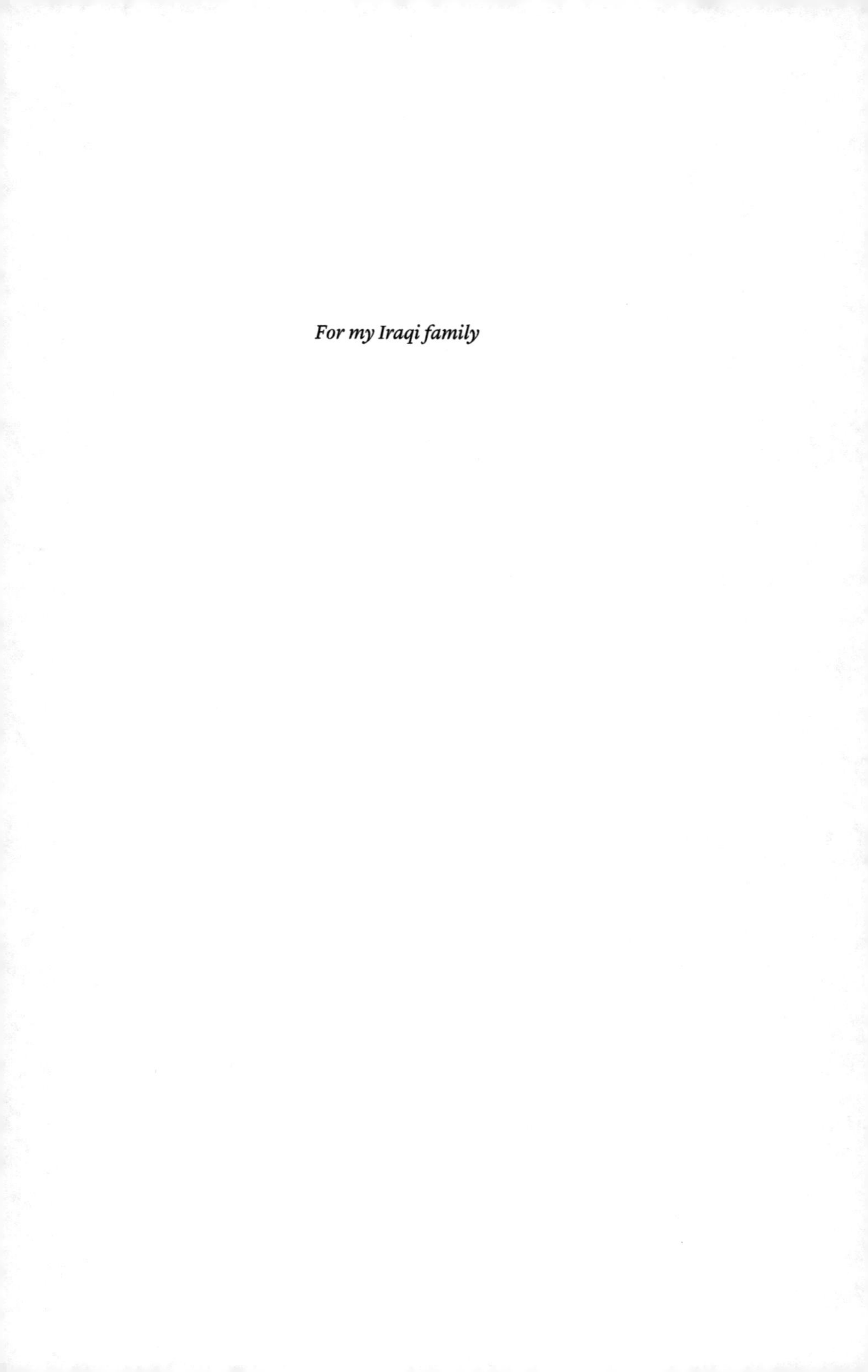

For my Iraqi family

The incapacity of Harun to restrain the followers of the Calf . . . was a wisdom from God made manifest in existence: that He be worshipped in every form.

MUHYI AL-DIN IBN ʿARABI

Democracy has no monuments. . . .
Its very essence is iconoclastic.

JOHN QUINCY ADAMS

Contents

Prologue

SOMETHING IS WRONG. It's February 26, 2015, and Iraqi-born art historian Zainab Bahrani has just completed a lecture at NYU's Institute for the Study of the Ancient World. From the audience comes a voice, asking with some urgency what can be done to save Mesopotamian antiquities from destruction. What has provoked the question? I retreat to a corner to check my phone, and there it is: a video of men smashing sculptures in Iraq's Mosul Museum, posted repeatedly on my feed.

A bearded man dressed in the black *taqiyah* and white *thawb* of a devout Muslim addresses the camera. He stands before a fragment of a large Assyrian sculpture known as a *lamassu*—a protective deity that combines a bull's body, an eagle's wings, and a human head.

"Oh Muslims, the remains that you see behind me are the idols of peoples of previous centuries, which were worshipped instead of God," the man explains in Arabic, with the poise of a museum docent. “The Prophet Muhammad commanded us to shatter and destroy statues. This is what his companions did when they conquered lands. Since God commanded us to shatter and destroy these statues, idols, and remains, it is easy for us to obey. We do not care what people think or if this costs us billions of dollars.”

When he finishes, the video transitions to a museum gallery. Three men topple a life-sized sculpture from its pedestal. Others look on. In the ensuing montage men overturn sculptures, smash them with sledgehammers, and mutilate them with pneumatic drills. For two and a half minutes, these images of destruction are interspersed with shots of decimated sculptures strewn across the floor—often rendered in slow motion, lending the sequence a lyrical quality.

The audio is no less carefully crafted: A lone voice chants a Qur᾿anic verse and then the sound of a *nashid* weaves through the duration of the video. In haunting tones, the Arabic song declares: “Demolish! Demolish! the state of idols / Hell is filled with idols and wood / Demolish the statues of America and its clan.” Even for those

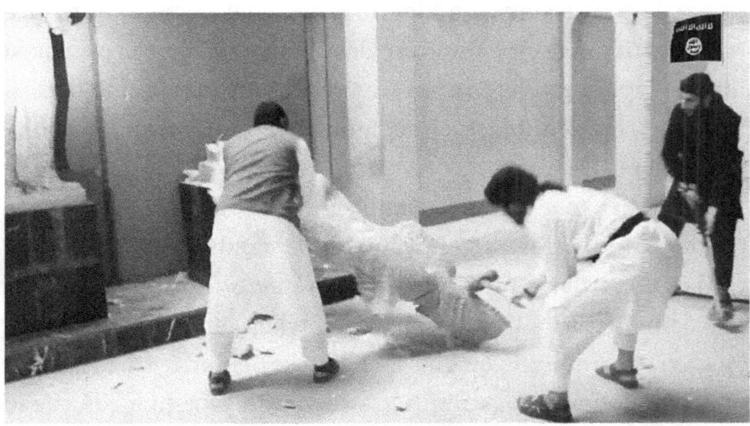

1. Islamic State destruction in the Mosul Museum, Iraq. Video released February 26, 2015.

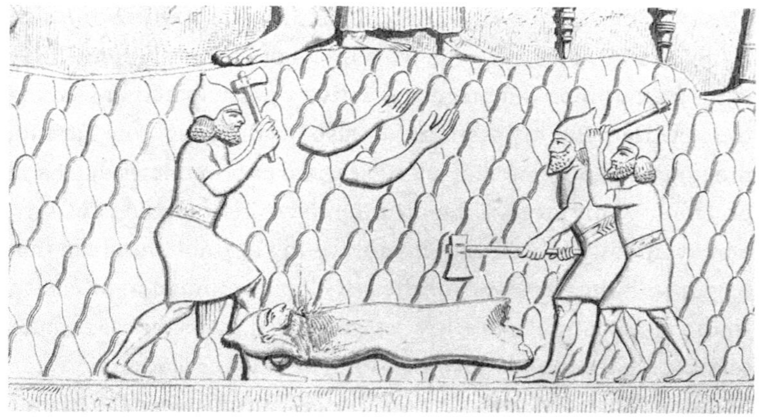

2. Three Assyrian soldiers smashing the sculpture of a king. Detail of a drawing by Eugène Flandin after a relief from Sargon II's palace at Khorsabad (eighth century BCE). Paul-Émile Botta, *Monument de Ninive*, 1849.

who cannot understand the lyrics, the music—punctuated by the sounds of shattering stone and machine-gun fire—is mesmerizing.

The video, I realized, bears an uncanny resemblance to a carved relief from the ancient Assyrian palace at Khorsabad, a town just north of Mosul. Both the video and the relief depict three men with sledgehammers smashing the toppled sculpture of a king (figures 1 and 2). What is there to say about these two images separated by more than twenty-five hundred years yet only fifteen miles? Why this persistent drive to destroy images—and to make other images showing their destruction?

●

This book grew out of a personal connection to the latest events tearing apart Iraq. My grandfather was born in Baghdad in 1910, eleven years before the establishment of the modern state. He belonged to a Jewish community that had called the banks of the Tigris home since antiquity, and he grew up among the bookstalls and literary cafés that now survive only in memoirs. (I recommend

Sasson Somekh's *Baghdad, Yesterday*.) This was a world in which Iraqi Jews lived side by side with Iraqis of other religions. They shared a common language and actively participated in shaping the new Iraq. But my grandfather also lived through the Farhud, the June 1941 pogrom that left nearly two hundred Jews dead and precipitated my family's departure—first to Tehran, then Tel Aviv, and eventually New York. The unraveling of Iraqi pluralism that began with the departure of the Jews has continued to intensify. In the aftermath of the 2003 American-led invasion, Baghdad's mixed neighborhoods gave way to rigorous segregation between Sunni and Shia. The forces of purity spread further when the Islamic State conquered Mosul in June 2014: Shia shrines were demolished; minority communities were butchered, enslaved, or made to flee their homes. The region seemed headed toward a homogeneity that it had not known since before the Tower of Babel.

In those foregone days after the flood, Genesis recounts, "The whole earth was one language, one set of words" (11:1). On the plains of Shinar, not far from modern Baghdad, all mankind sought to build "a city and a tower with its top in the heavens" in order to remain united. With technological prowess, they set to work baking mud into bricks. But God frustrated the plan by confounding their language such that they could no longer speak in one voice. The project came to a halt and the people dispersed.

On first reading, the biblical story seems antagonistic to the means and aims of political life. God opposes the human aspiration to live together in a city. But deeper scrutiny suggests that the people weren't really building a *political* city.

Politics presupposes plurality. It's a strategy for reconciling opposing opinions and interests that grows out of a need to live together despite our different perspectives on the world. It attests to our ability to overcome differences without recourse to violence. Doing so is difficult, and often isn't pretty. It's what Max Weber famously called "a strong and slow boring of hard boards."[1] By contrast, the biblical story imagines a time when mankind didn't need politics. Already speaking as one, the people aspired only to prevent future dissent. Their city would be, not a political arena, but an infrastructure for enforcing unity. Babel's builders built in the hopes of securing a world without politics.

Aristotle understood this all too human desire and warned against it. "By advancing in unity, a political community will eventually cease being a political community," he writes in the *Politics*. "As if one were to turn harmony into mere unison or rhythm into a single beat."[2] If we could become as unified as Babel's builders supposedly were, Aristotle implies, we'd no longer be political. We'd no longer need to be. Despite perpetual illusions to the contrary, this wouldn't leave us better off. It would be a form of slavery. Instead we should cultivate our capacity for politics, and this requires understanding images.

The public space in which politics occurs is never unadorned. It is shaped by images that influence how we perceive the world—forming our desires and imbuing us with shared values and ideals. The images may be paintings, sculptures, and photographs, or movies, television shows, video games, and memes. (Though literature likewise shapes our commitments—and there are important parallels between iconoclasm and censorship—I don't focus on verbal image-making in this book.) Without such shared images, the political plurality that Aristotle likens to harmony would produce only cacophony. We'd be locked into irreconcilable individuality, incapable of projects that require collective vision. And yet, dangers arise if images take too strong a hold on people's minds. They can polarize us into factions incapable of communicating with one another or reduce us to a unity that speaks with a tyrant's single voice. Politics needs both images and a citizenry capable of evaluating them critically.

The same month ISIS released the Mosul Museum video, its online magazine *Dabiq* featured a twelve-page article titled "The Extinction of the Grayzone."[3] It describes the group's intention to divide the world into two camps "with no third in between." Space for doubt, moderation, and compromise must be abolished. Islamic State images are purposefully brutal; they seek to compel people to take sides. The fully polarized world ISIS imagines will have "no place for grayish calls and movements. There will only be the camp of *iman* [faith] versus the camp of *kufr* [apostasy]." In other words, there will be no place for politics. For it is only in "gray zones" that productive dialogue and debate can occur. Gray zones coincide with what political philosopher Hannah Arendt called the public realm. To retain the freedom that Arendt argued emerges with politics, we must cultivate gray zones, not eradicate them. But how do we withstand images that seek to polarize us? And what kinds of images might instead nurture the gray zone of politics?

I first watched the Mosul Museum video on Facebook. Hailed as democratizing political access, online platforms have also been accused of entrapping us in homogeneous echo chambers where we all share "one language and one speech." Far from offering up the world in its plurality, social media generates a plurality of worlds. Algorithms distort our experience of the public realm.

In her book *Alone Together*, Sherry Turkle concludes that technology makes us "forget our human purposes."[4] Though her work focuses on loss of privacy, its implications for the public realm are equally worrying. People happily use technology to flee face-to-face conversations, Turkle observes, "because face-to-face conversations are difficult." Technology offers to make interactions easier. It seduces us with "the idea of a relational world that might be 'friction free,' kind of like the machine world."

But politics will never be friction free, and political action can't be algorithmic. Politics is messy. That's why it has always been tempting to flee the demands of politics by abnegating responsibility to a superior force—God, History, the Market, and now the Algorithm. This longing to escape the mess of politics echoes in the iconoclast's hammer.

While Moses was busy speaking with God on Mount Sinai, his brother Aaron made an image to guide the recently emancipated Israelites. Moses demands an explanation. "I flung [gold] into the fire," Aaron tells him, "and out came this calf" (Exodus 32:24). Aaron's denial of agency illustrates a common anxiety about authoritative images: we do not want to take responsibility for how they orient us in the world. Outsourcing that responsibility makes life easier. Men like Moses can't abide such chicanery; they know that images are the work of human hands. This doesn't make Moses any more open to political life than his duplicitous brother. His aversion to the Golden Calf cannot be appeased by correcting its false attribution. He seeks a truly transcendent authority. Each brother, in his own way, wants to escape human responsibility for political life. Neither makes room for politics as a human endeavor, or the manmade images that necessarily come with it.

Moses's aversion makes idolatry difficult to circumscribe. Idols don't have a particular form or content that we can simply identify, isolate, and annihilate, leaving all other images intact. Any image can be perceived as an idol, whether in a positive sense—a standard worthy of orienting human life—or a negative sense: an impostor encroaching on the transcendent. Law can deem some images illicit, but not without other images enabling its authority.

In his opera *Moses und Aron*, twentieth-century composer Arnold Schoenberg reimagines the scene between the two brothers. Unlike his biblical namesake, Schoenberg's Aaron doesn't deny his own agency in making the Calf. Rather, he challenges his brother's idea that God's law can be established without images. Moses himself uses images, Aaron points out. When Moses destroys the Calf with an utterance, the destruction serves as an image for the people. And the Tablets of the Law that Moses holds, Aaron asserts, are no less an image. When Moses then smashes the tablets in despair, the violent act is just one more image. Recognizing his inability to escape images, Moses collapses on stage, wailing, "O word, thou word, that I lack!"[5] The opera continues with a final act in which a reinvigorated Moses condemns Aaron for betraying the idea to the image, but Schoenberg never composed music for the scenes following Moses's collapse. We, like Moses, the opera attests, can never escape images. Iconoclasm itself engenders them.

Which brings me back to the Mosul Museum video. While some in the video wield hammers, others point cameras, generating new images including the video itself. What does this video reveal about the role images play in politics? Why destroy images? Can we find better ways to live together in their midst? I will probe these questions over three chapters. First, I consider the claim that the sculptures in the Mosul Museum were idols that must be destroyed. Next, I explore the significance of the museum as a setting. And finally, I take up the fact that the destruction was recorded in order to be seen. Though the ISIS videographers may have wanted to shock, their video can help us think.

1

Idols

WHEN MUHAMMAD conquered Mecca he set about cleansing the Ka'ba shrine of idols. An authoritative tradition reports, "The Prophet entered Mecca and there were three hundred and sixty idols around the Ka'ba. He started stabbing the idols with a stick he had in his hand and reciting: 'Truth has come and falsehood has vanished.'"[1] Though not recounted in the Qur'an, the story of Muhammad smashing the idols of the Meccans has become commonplace, appearing in Ibn al-Kalbi's ninth-century *Book of Idols* and in popular biographies of the Prophet. When the ISIS spokesman in the Mosul Museum video informs viewers that "the Prophet Muhammad shattered the idols with his own honorable hands when he conquered Mecca," he appeals to precedent. He imagines cleansing the Mosul Museum as a reenactment of the moment of Islamic origins. The smashing of idols belongs to the Islamic State's larger program: the revival of an original time of purity.

In fact, it is a reenactment of a reenactment. Just as ISIS hearkens back to Muhammad, Islamic tradition presents Muhammad as having revived the ways of Ibrahim. Throughout the Qur'an, Muhammad speaks of restoring the faith of Ibrahim, which had been corrupted over the intervening centuries. "Ibrahim was neither a Jew nor a Christian," the Qur'an attests. "He was upright and a submitter [*muslim*], never an idolater" (3:67).° One way Ibrahim demonstrated his submission was to obey God's command to build the Ka'ba shrine. The Qur'an recounts how God "showed Ibrahim the site of the House, saying, 'Do not assign partners to Me. Purify My House for those who circle around it, those who stand to pray, and those who bow and prostrate themselves'" (22:26). The idols that Muhammad smashes had been brought into the holy precinct after Ibrahim's death. By cleansing the shrine, Muhammad aims to restore the Ka'ba to its earlier purity.

It is no surprise, then, that as the ISIS video transitions from prologue to main action it cites Ibrahim smashing the idols. A snippet of the Qur'an appears on-screen: "He reduced them to fragments." Here's the passage in full:

> Ibrahim said to his father and his people, "What are these images to which you are so devoted?" They replied, "We found our fathers serving them." He said, "You and your fathers have clearly gone astray."

°The Arabic word *muslim*—"one who submits"—designates the appropriate way of comporting oneself toward God. According to renowned Islamist Ignaz Goldziher, "The word expresses, first and foremost, a feeling of dependency on an unbounded omnipotence to which man must submit and resign his will. It expresses, better than any other, Muhammad's idea of the relation between the believer and the object of his worship." And yet, as Shahab Ahmed rightly insists in *What Is Islam?*, the working out of the act of *islam* has taken varied and contradictory forms over the centuries. Putting the ideal into practice has always required creatively imagining submission in a form that accords with the necessities of human life.

> They asked, "Have you brought us the truth or are you just playing about?" He said, "Listen! Your true lord is the lord of the heavens and the earth, he who created them, and I am a witness to this. By God I shall certainly outwit your idols as soon as you have turned your backs!" He reduced them to fragments, but left the biggest one for them to return to. They said, "Who has done this to our gods? How wicked he must be!" Some said, "We heard a youth called Ibrahim talking about them." They said, "Bring him before the eyes of the people, so that they may witness [his trial]." They asked, "Was it you, Ibrahim, who did this to our gods?" He said, "No, it was done by the biggest of them—this one. Ask them, if they can talk." . . . They said, "You know very well these gods can't speak." Ibrahim said, "How can you serve what can neither benefit nor harm you, instead of God? Shame on you and the things you serve instead of God. Have you no sense?" (21:52–67)[2]

The video alludes to this story only through the momentary on-screen appearance of that single line: "He reduced them to fragments." But an article published in *Dabiq*, the Islamic State's online magazine, soon after the video was released makes the connection explicit. "Erasing the Legacy of a Ruined Nation" celebrates how "the soldiers of the Khalifah, with sledgehammers in hand, revived the Sunnah of their father Ibrahim (*ʿalayhis-salam*) when they laid waste to the *shirki* [idolatrous] legacy of a nation that had long passed from the face of the Earth."[3] The article favorably compares the destruction not only to Ibrahim's act but also to his attitude. Dismissing outrage about the destruction of ancient cultural heritage, it explains that the Islamic State's fighters "were not the least bit concerned about the feelings and sentiments of the *kuffar* [unbelievers], just as Ibrahim was not concerned about the feelings and sentiments of his people when he destroyed their idols."

Like Ibrahim, determined to cleanse the world of idols—violently, if necessary—ISIS would pay no heed to contemporary censures.

Ibrahim leaves the largest idol standing. If Ibrahim intended merely to destroy idols, why would he do this? As the rest of the story makes clear, smashing the idols' bodies appears to have been only the first act in a well-calibrated performance aimed at changing minds. Unlike ISIS, Ibrahim is much concerned with his neighbors' thinking. He seeks to free the minds of his contemporaries, but adolescent that he is, his ploy betrays a certain naïveté.

The story begins with Ibrahim asking the people about the images to which they appear so devoted. The people, evincing a conservative practical wisdom, tell him they serve the images as their fathers did. Though the verb *ʿibada* is often translated as "worship" when used with reference to gods, its basic meaning is "to serve"—as a slave serves a master or a subject serves a king. If we resist our modern tendency to consign religion and politics to separate, autonomous spheres, we will be better attuned to the term's political connotations. The images the people serve are intimately connected to the political regime under which they live: to "serve images" (the literal meaning of the Greek *idol-latria*, idolatry) is to serve the sovereign who rules through them. By advocating submission to "your true lord, the lord of the heavens and the earth," Ibrahim does not simply criticize the people's theology; he subverts their politics. He is calling for regime change.

It is significant that the Qurʾanic story uses the terms "image" and "idol" interchangeably. Ibrahim makes no distinction between the two. His anxiety applies not only to some subset of images considered illicit—that is, "idols"—but to images generally. Why? Because Ibrahim knows that all images fall short of the truth. And so he rejects them all. He leaves no room for a regime to sidestep the problem of political images by claiming that its images (as opposed to others') are true. If all images are false, any politics grounded in images will be idolatrous. To avoid idolatry, Ibrahim demands a regime without images.°

When ISIS went on its rampage in the Mosul Museum, many accused the group of hypocrisy since videos, too, are images. If ISIS were sincere in its opposition to idolatry, this line of reasoning maintained, it wouldn't visually record members' iconoclastic acts. Some scholars responded casuistically that Islamic law permits video but not sculpture. Treating idolatry as a legal issue, however, fails to recognize the depth of the problem as Ibrahim presents it. Juristic debate about the illicit status of a particular kind of image (called an "idol") presupposes allegiance to the law itself. Such allegiance, I shall argue, cannot exist without other images that provide the law's foundation. Ibrahim worries that the images that ground the law get in the way of submission to God.

•

Islamic exegetical tradition embroiders the political context of Ibrahim's iconoclasm, which is only hinted at in the Qurʾan. In his *History of Prophets and Kings*, the polymath Muhammad ibn Jarir al-Tabari (839–923) collects numerous traditional accounts that set the story during the reign of Nimrud—the legendary king of Baby-

°The Christian tradition of Veronica's veil seeks a way around Ibrahim's equation of images and idols. Folk etymology derives the saint's name from the Latin word *vera*, meaning "true," and the Greek *eikon*, another word for "image." Veronica is said to have wiped Christ's brow with her veil as he was carrying his cross to Golgotha, and the image of his face became miraculously imprinted on it. The impression is argued to be a "true image" because it came into being without human mediation—as an *acheiropoieton*, literally "not made by hands." This attempt to save the truth of images by denying their human manufacture echoes Aaron's claim that the Golden Calf simply emerged from the fire. Like Moses, Ibrahim isn't impressed by such subtleties.

lon, associated in the popular imagination with the monumental Mesopotamian civilizations.

As al-Tabari reports, astrologers tell Nimrud that "a boy will be born in this city of yours who will be called Ibrahim. He will abandon your religion and break your idols."[4] Nimrud responds by commanding that in the foretold month every newborn boy be killed. Yet Ibrahim survives and lives to fulfill the prophecy. When Ibrahim is found guilty of destroying the idols, Nimrud tries once more to execute him—this time by burning him alive. That attempt, too, fails, and an astounded Nimrud declares his willingness to offer a sacrifice to Ibrahim's god. "God will not accept anything from you as long as you keep any vestige of this old religion of yours," Ibrahim tells the king. "You must leave it for my religion."[5]

Nimrud's reply is revealing: "O Ibrahim! I cannot abandon my kingship, but I will slaughter the cattle for Him." Nimrud understands that the idols constituted a fundamental feature of his regime: abandoning his religion would be equivalent to forsaking his position as king (an equivalence implied earlier when the astrologers refer to "your idols" and "your religion" rather than "our idols" and "our religion"). Though impressed by Ibrahim's god, Nimrud is not prepared to dismantle his regime.

Ibrahim wishes to replace a regime that relies on images with one that does not. His imageless regime will be grounded in the logic of creation. "Your true lord is the lord of the heavens and the earth, he who created them," he tells the townspeople, "and I am a witness to this." If the people would forsake their idols, he believes, they too could relate directly to nature's God, and serve without the mediation of human-made images.

What gives Ibrahim the impression that such a regime is possible? Accounts of his early childhood suggest an intriguing answer. Al-Tabari reports that to avoid Nimrud's murderous scheme, Ibrahim's mother gave birth to him and raised him in a cave. Unlike the cave in Plato's allegory in the *Republic*—which stands for life within the city, subject to the city's images—Ibrahim's cave shelters him from receiving a political education. Upon leaving the cave as a young adult, Ibrahim looked at the world and deduced that only the creator of the heavens and the earth could be the true lord. Unaffected by the political commitments Nimrud's regime inculcates through its idols, he is, al-Tabari writes, "free of the religion of his people" and thus free to imagine an alternative.

But is Ibrahim's "regime without images" feasible? His neighbors remain rightly skeptical.

●

Abu Nasr al-Farabi (ca. 870–950) thought deeply about the relation between images and politics. A younger contemporary of al-Tabari, al-Farabi was born in Central Asia, on the periphery of the Islamic world, but spent much of his adult life in Baghdad—the cosmopolitan center of the Abbasid Caliphate so colorfully depicted in the pages of *The Arabian Nights*. He seems also to have traveled to Byzantine lands, possibly to Constantinople itself, to study Greek philosophy with Christian scholars who had inherited the traditions of the Hellenistic philosophical schools. Al-Farabi wrote numerous works on topics such as logic, politics, and music theory. While "all his writings are faultlessly excellent" (as the Jewish philosopher Maimonides wrote in 1199) his political treatises in particular shed light on Ibrahim's iconoclasm.

Al-Farabi adapted the insights of ancient political philosophers—especially Plato and Aristotle—to make sense of prophetic religion. Although the Greek philosophers had never encountered prophetic religion in its fleshed-out monotheistic form, their writings provided a basis for understanding prophetic religion as fundamentally political—concerned with establishing the conditions under which human beings can harmoniously live together. As al-Farabi writes in

The Attainment of Happiness, "an isolated individual cannot achieve all the perfections by himself and without the aid of many other individuals."[6] Such mutual assistance rests on agreement about what is good and what is evil. Left to themselves, individuals of differing appetites, faculties, and experiences won't naturally arrive at such agreement. If a political community is to take shape—and if it does not, al-Farabi warns, human happiness is impossible—individuals' natural inclinations will have to be redirected so that their opinions become shared. Religion, al-Farabi teaches, is what makes this possible.

"Religion is opinions and actions," al-Farabi writes in his *Book of Religion*, "determined and restricted with stipulations and prescribed for a community by their first ruler."[7] This definition is thoroughly political. Religion, for al-Farabi, concerns not merely that part of life set apart as sacred (as we might define it today) but rather that which determines what is considered sacred in the first place. When applied to Islam, al-Farabi's definition of religion emphasizes the Prophet's great accomplishment as a lawgiver: establishing a community by instituting shared opinions about the good and designating actions that conform to it. But the definition does not restrict itself to Islam; all political communities with shared opinions and actions possess religion in al-Farabi's sense. They, too, have prophet-lawgivers.

How does a prophet-lawgiver establish religion in a polity? This is where images come into play.

Most of us don't think about matters in purely abstract or conceptual terms. Our opinions often take the form of images. We model our actions on concrete examples of virtue, justice, and beauty. So a religion that strives for consonance among citizens cannot impart its teachings solely by means of abstract concepts. Instead, the prophet-lawgiver must invent compelling images. Thanks to his well-honed imaginative faculty (it is the excellence of this very faculty that distinguishes him as a prophet), the prophet-lawgiver creates images that help citizens "imagine everything that is in the city—kings, rulers, and servants; their ranks, the relation between them, and their subordination to one another."[8] He converts theoretical knowledge of natural and political things into descriptions that seize the imaginations of ordinary people—descriptions of God and the universe, prophets and kings, saints and sinners. Such images offer members of a polity a common understanding of nature, morality, and human happiness.

Images superimpose a layer of collective meaning on a natural world that could not otherwise sustain political life. Without the political "second nature" that images inculcate in us nearly from birth, allegiance to an otherwise abstract and impersonal law would be impossible. The law on its own isn't lovable. It is through images that we come to identify with what the law stands for and protects. "For traditional laws to become firmly established in the hearts of the inhabitants of the city," al-Farabi writes in his *Summary of Plato's Laws*, "preludes must be made prior to setting them down."[9] Just as a prelude introduces and sets the tone for the main musical work, prophetic images prepare citizens to accept and adhere to the law. Images provide the foundation on which the law is built. Through images, the solitary world of an individual face to face with unmediated nature becomes a common world of shared expectations and aspirations in which law can take root. Images, in short, are what make political life possible.

The evocation of music raises the question of what counts as an image. Al-Farabi's discussion encompasses both visual and literary representations. An epic poem about heroic deeds counts as an image just as much as a painting depicting the same subject. I would argue that his account of images even applies to the non-mimetic arts. Arabesque design and the muezzin's call do more than decorate a building or tell a person when to pray; they cultivate particular moods and create an environment—visual or aural—that multiple individuals can collectively identify as their own. The prophet-lawgiver has all of these arts at his disposal. Those who claim that Islamic law does not depend on human-made images do not conceive of images broadly enough; al-Farabi was able to adapt Plato's image-making lawgiver to his Islamic world because he knew that even the most emphatic disavowal of images cannot sustain itself politically without deploying other images.

So the fact that regimes regularly prohibit images should not distract from the more basic point: the legal proscription of images depends on images. Laws proscribing images presuppose other images already grounding those laws. Al-Farabi's assertion that preludes must be made *prior to* setting down the law nicely captures this necessity. Ibrahim's "regime without images" could only come into being if it used images to cultivate a commitment to its law of no images.

●

As the externalized form of communal longings and ideals, prophetic images hold the power to bind a community together and inspire a shared conception of the good. Without images, the townspeople whose idols Ibrahim shatters could not survive as a community. Despite Ibrahim's assertion that their images "can neither benefit nor harm" them, those images are hardly impotent. Elsewhere in the Qur'an, he appears to admit as much.

Ibrahim tells the people, "You have only taken to yourselves idols, apart from God, as a mark of mutual love between you in the present life; then upon the Day of Resurrection you will deny one another, and you will curse one another, and your refuge will be the Fire, and you will have no helpers" (29:25). Ibrahim objects to images, then, not because they are powerless, but because they exert the wrong kind of power. They direct the people's concern to the present earthly world rather than the world to come. He predicts that communal cohesion will dissolve on the Day of Resurrection—precisely when political life as we know it comes to an end. This reinforces the conclusion that the people's images *do* work under present circumstances. But from Ibrahim's eschatological perspective, that work is counterproductive. His frightening talk of hellfire aims to persuade the people to abandon images that direct their attention to their well-being in the present world. Of course, Ibrahim doesn't admit that hell itself is an image. Consciously or not, he substitutes new images (which direct attention to the world to come) for old ones (which focus on the here-and-now).°

Whether a set of images is beneficial or harmful depends on whether the goal, imagined as a common good, is actually good. Images may be powerful and yet harmful. Alluding to the "age of ignorance" (*jahiliyya*) said to have preceded Islam, al-Farabi calls a city founded on harmful images an ignorant regime.•

° Thomas Hobbes sought a similar substitution, but in reverse. The English philosopher (or, perhaps better, prophet-lawgiver) took aim at the images of traditional Christianity that promote fear of "eternal torments" in order to instill the belief, on which he understood modern politics to rest, that there is no greater evil than violent death. Hobbes considered the old images detrimental to his concept of sovereignty. "It is impossible that a commonwealth should stand, where any other than the sovereign, hath a power of giving greater rewards than life, and of inflicting greater punishments than death . . . and *eternal torment* [is] a greater punishment than the *death of nature*" (*Leviathan*, chap. 38). Hobbes makes clear that fear of eternal torment depends on images of hell since "there is no natural knowledge of man's estate after death" (*Leviathan*, chap. 15); he is less explicit about the extent to which his own axiom, that fear of violent death is the greatest evil, also relies on images, such as those he uses to paint life in the state of nature as "nasty, brutish, and short."

• In Islamic tradition, the *jahiliyya* preceded God's revelation to Muhammad. Al-Farabi removes that temporal connotation, applying the term to any polity that falls short of the ideal virtuous city. According to his *Political Regime*, the *jahili* city is one that cares only for bodily necessities, focuses on pleasure (hedonism), strives after wealth (plutocracy) or honor (timocracy), prioritizes domination, or rules itself democratically.

What is unsettling about Ibrahim is not his opposition to Nimrud's regime so much as his denial of politics. Since no political regime can exist without images, the critic's task is to evaluate the images a regime employs—not simply to denounce the fact that it employs them. Ibrahim, however, refuses to recognize the prerequisites of politics. Though his opposition to Nimrud's rule is rooted in a commendable concern for truth, his impulse to trump the king by appealing to God's superior power risks shattering the possibility of human politics, which remains our only access to justice, however imperfect.

Al-Tabari reports a conversation between Nimrud and Ibrahim that illuminates this game of one-upmanship:

> Then Nimrud said to Ibrahim, "Have you seen this God whom you serve and to whose service you call others, and of whose power you speak, and whom you glorify above any other? Who is He?" Ibrahim replied to him, "My Lord, who gives life and causes death." And Nimrud said, "I, too, give life and cause death." Ibrahim asked, "How do you give life and death?" He replied, "I shall take two men—two were condemned to death by my order—and I'll kill one of them, so I will have caused him to die, and I'll pardon the other and free him, so I will have made him live." But upon hearing that, Ibrahim said to him, "God causes the sun to rise in the East, so can you make it rise in the West?" Knowing that it was as Ibrahim said, *the disbeliever was dumbfounded* and he gave no answer; he knew that he was not able to do that.[10]

Ibrahim assumes that sovereignty belongs to the most powerful. Simply put, if God is more powerful than Nimrud, then God deserves to rule. The question of what regime might best suit conflicting demands for justice is never raised. Instead of being dumbfounded by Ibrahim's appeal to God's supernatural power, Nimrud might have replied that to demand that a ruler change the course of nature is to misunderstand the scope of political power.

So, too, to demand that a ruler rule without recourse to images. If images are a prerequisite for producing willing obedience to the law, then rule without images implies rule by force alone. The exegetical tradition is wrong to present Nimrud as a tyrant simply because he used idols to rule. By using images, Nimrud's regime sought to cultivate willing obedience among the population and thus avoid reducing politics to the mere exercise of force. Of course, tyrants also exploit the power of images—but that doesn't make images the mark of tyranny.

And yet, even without knowing the substance of Nimrud's images, their pervasiveness raises alarms. The sources tell us that the king of Babylon ruled over the entire earth. Were Nimrud's images well suited to all of mankind? Both the nature of human beings and the nature of images suggest otherwise. In *Political Regime*, al-Farabi remarks that any group of people necessarily develops distinguishing characteristics due to its particular historical and geographical situation. People are never blank slates when a prophet arrives, and so the prophet must invent images that correspond to the distinctive character of the group for whom he legislates. Truth must be "represented to each group or nation by things of which they are more cognizant."[11] Images adequate to inspire Britons—an island people with a history of common law and naval empire—would be ineffective for a group of nomadic Bedouin or Tyrolean mountaineers.

For an image to be truly universal, it would have to speak to a part of us that we unchangingly share with all other human beings—and only that part. Our basic bodily needs might serve as such a common denominator. But what of loftier communal aspirations? Because these normally take form in conjunction with a group's distinctive characteristics, an image meant to be universal must leave them aside. A regime that aspires to ground its rule in universally applicable images risks failing to address people's deepest desires and hopes, leading to alienation and perhaps even revolt. At worst, such a regime would try to eradicate distinctive characteristics in order to produce a homogenous population.°

The nature of images similarly suggests that a world-state is inadvisable. According to al-Farabi, although the truth is "one and immutable, the things by which [it is] represented are many and different."[12] Images, as approximations of the truth, are multiple. None is exhaustive. Because images must emphasize some aspects of a thing at the expense of others, alternative representations are always possible. "Therefore," he writes, "it is possible to represent [the truth] to one group and one nation by objects other than those by which they are represented to another group and another nation. Thus it may be possible for the religions of virtuous nations and virtuous cities to differ even if they all pursue the very same happiness."[13] Al-Farabi thus argues, not only for the multiplicity of images, but for the possibility of multiple, equally legitimate religions.

Only the truth, al-Farabi maintains, is properly universal. But

°Al-Farabi addresses the idea of a world-state directly in *Principles of the Opinions of the Inhabitants of the Virtuous City*, as part of a catalogue of opinions about what holds communities together. After listing such options as shared territory, shared lineage, and shared language, he considers the claim that our shared humanity unites us. Proponents of this view assert that only different species engage in war. All mankind ought to live in peace, they conclude, because all men belong to the common species "man." Political divisions exist only because some people persist in acting against nature, trying to overcome other men with force. Those who want to unite humanity in accord with nature must therefore establish an army to suppress those who rise up against nature. Al-Farabi includes the proponents of this view among those he calls "ignorant of the true good."

the truth itself cannot ground a political order. Images used by a regime with universal pretensions would necessarily fall short of the universality that they claim. They would always be vulnerable to challenge from alternate images. To remain in power, the ruler of any regime with universal pretentions would have to use force to suppress challenges to the regime's claim to universality.

What about God's universal rule? According to Ibrahim, serving God doesn't entail idolatry because the creator of heaven and earth does not rule the world through images. The earnest enlightener seems unaware of the implications of his position. If God doesn't rule through images, then he must resort to force. Ibrahim's imagined ideal renders consent irrelevant and politics impossible. Human beings would, at best, submit as automatically to God's rule as plants and animals do. At worst, we would suffer under a superhuman tyranny far greater than any mortal has been able to devise. Nimrud's regime, however tyrannical, looks good by comparison.

The story of Ibrahim has served Muslims as a powerful image throughout the history of Islam. Nonetheless, it is important not to confuse the regime Ibrahim imagines in the Qur᾿anic story with the religion as it has been practiced.

Al-Farabi rarely refers to the particulars of one religion or another, yet his view on images takes on particular significance when read with Islamic tradition in mind. In *Political Regime*, he writes:

> Most people who pursue happiness pursue what is imagined, not what they form a concept of. Similarly, the principles such as are to be accepted, imitated, extolled, and exalted are accepted by most people as they imagine them, not as they form a concept of them. Those who pursue happiness as they form a concept of it and accept the principles as they form a concept of them are the wise, whereas those in whose souls these things are found as they are imagined

and who accept them and pursue them as though they are like that are the believers.[14]

The juxtaposition of the wise and the believers is unusual here. Al-Farabi usually contrasts the wise with the vulgar masses. "Believers" (*mu'minin*) is the standard term for Muhammad's followers in the Qur'an—where it appears over a hundred times, and its cognates (like the verb "to believe") many hundreds more. By calling those who rely upon images for their happiness "the believers," al-Farabi signals that reliance upon images—including images of God—applies as well to Islam. His comment implies that the heroes of the Qur'an and those who have followed them have themselves never submitted to God without the mediation of images.

Ibrahim in the story may be naïve, but the story of Ibrahim is not. If believers believe they can serve God without the mediation of images, it is prophetic images that help them to do so. The story of Ibrahim and the idolaters is itself one such image. Whether disseminated verbally or visually (as in figure 3), this image of image destruction allows believers to imagine themselves, like Ibrahim, rejecting images that obstruct direct submission to God. The story instills the belief that life without images is possible. This belief is reinforced by other images: "The most grievously tormented people among the denizens of hell on the Day of Resurrection will be the makers of images," announces one *hadith*.[15] Since this punishment would be manifestly unjust if images were necessary for human life, the *hadith* propagates the belief that life without images is possible. It does so by making an image of hell. These are images that cultivate a forgetting of images.

The story of Ibrahim and the *hadith*'s image of hell belong to a larger field of prophetic images that have helped establish Islam as a form of communal life over the centuries. Rather than offer-

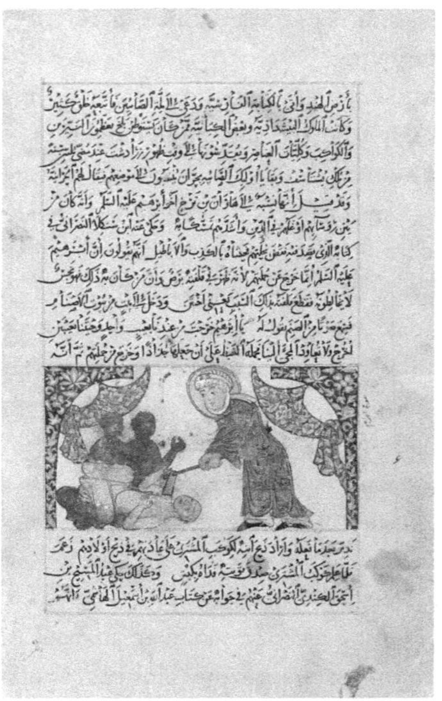

3. Ibrahim smashing the idols. Al-Biruni, *Chronology of Ancient Nations*, f.88v. Iran or northern Iraq, 1307. University of Edinburgh.

ing believers a path to God devoid of images, the Qur᾽an and subsequent Islamic traditions provide their adherents with new images in place of older ones. Only with images can Islam be political. And yet, false prophets still periodically arise with seductive visions of a world unsullied by the realities that come with being political beings.

●

"Demolish! Demolish! the state of idols," repeats the chanted *nashid* that accompanies the video of destruction in the Mosul Museum. When Ibrahim smashed the people's idols, Nimrud understood the performance as a direct attack on his sovereignty. Whose sovereignty is ISIS targeting?

The spokesman in the video somewhat inaccurately identifies the images under attack as having belonged to "the Assyrians, Akkadians, and others." Though he doesn't name Nimrud, it is tempting to see these ancient Mesopotamian objects through the lens of Islamic tradition as belonging to Nimrud's kingdom. This clarifies the video as a symbol of the Islamic State's obsession with reenacting the past, but it also leaves open the question of the political target. Nimrud and his kingdom are long vanished; what good comes from attacking the images of a defunct regime?

Later, the video's *nashid* suggests a contemporary adversary: "Demolish the statues of America and its clan," the song intones. It comes as no surprise that ISIS would target the United States "and its clan," but in what sense can ancient Mesopotamian sculpture be considered American?

The term *jahiliyya* might encode an answer. In its most constricted sense, the term refers to the century or so of Arabian history that predates the arrival of Muhammad. The era is best remembered for its highly stylized poetry celebrating the virtues of kin, lampooning enemies, recalling lost loves, and lamenting the dead. (The *nashid* that accompanies the Mosul Museum video has roots in this traditional poetry, which, as Robyn Creswell and Bernard Haykel describe, ISIS militants rework to "articulate the fantasy life of jihad.")[16] With time, the term's meaning expanded to include the epoch before the establishment of Islam. In this sense, as peoples of the pre-Islamic past "the Assyrians, Akkadians, and others" belong to the period of *jahiliyya*.

The term's meaning has broadened in other ways too. As we have seen, al-Farabi used it to refer to any regime that falls short of the virtuous city—regardless of its chronological place in history. Thinkers like Ibn Taymiyya (1263–1328) and Ibn ʿAbd al-Wahhab

(1703–1792) used the term to censure what they saw as the persistence of pre-Islamic customs among the Muslims of their own day. In modern times, the reformers Muhammad ʿAbduh (1849–1905) and Rashid Rida (1865–1935) also compared aspects of contemporary Muslim life with aspects of *jahili* society. A. Yusuf ʿAli (d. 1953), in a gloss on the word *jahiliyya* in his English translation of the Qurʾan, comments, "The Days of Ignorance were the days of tribalism, feuds, and selfish accentuation of differences in man. Those days are not really yet over. It is the mission of Islam to take us away from that false mental attitude."[17] In the 1960s, Sayyid Qutb (1906–1966), whose writings remain influential in radical circles to this day, popularized the term *jahiliyya* in his attempt to articulate what is wrong with modern life.

Born in a village in Upper Egypt, Qutb participated in Cairo's literary scene from the mid-1920s through the early 1950s. Repulsed by the loose mores he encountered during a government-sponsored study trip in the United States, Qutb began to develop the hard-line brand of Islam for which he is best known. Returning to Egypt, Qutb joined the Muslim Brotherhood. He became a fierce critic of the Egyptian government and the lingering influence of the imperial powers despite the country's nominal independence. When the Muslim Brotherhood failed in an attempt on the life of Egyptian president Gamal Nasser in 1954, the group was banned and Qutb imprisoned. He spent most of the rest of his life in jail, where he wrote a massive Qurʾanic commentary called *In the Shade of the Qurʾan*; his best-known book, *Milestones*, which is a call for Islamic revolution; and numerous other works. In 1966 he was executed for plotting against the Egyptian government. (As Roxanne Euben has suggested, Qutb's heroic life story—with its conversion narrative and martyrdom—has played an important role in fostering commitment to his ideas.)

Jahiliyya is a central concept in Qutb's more radical later writings. A society that fails to follow God's guidance in all areas of life, he argues, is *jahili* and engaged in the usurpation of divine sovereignty. *Jahili* societies are human-made imposter sovereignties—whether they take the form of tribes, clans, kingdoms, empires, or, today, nation-states. "The true character of Islam," he writes in *Milestones*, "is a universal proclamation of the freedom of man from servitude to other men, the establishment of the sovereignty of God and His Lordship throughout the world, the end of man's arrogance and selfishness, and the implementation of the divine law in human affairs."[18]

In his commentary on the Qur᾽an, Qutb elaborates: "*Jahiliyya* means that people are ruled by people, because this signifies that they submit to one another. They refuse to submit to God alone and reject His Godhead, acknowledging instead that some human beings have qualities of Godhead and hence they submit to their authority." Qutb insists that *jahiliyya* is not a time but a condition: "In all ages and places, people may implement God's law, yielding no part of it for any reason, submitting to it willingly. As such, they follow the religion chosen for them by God. Alternatively, they may acknowledge and implement a man-made law in any shape or form. As such they follow ignorance."[19]

As objects dating to the historical *jahiliyya*, the artifacts in the Mosul Museum function as emblems of *jahiliyya* in its nonhistorical sense. As objects in a museum, they contribute to instituting *jahiliyya* in its modern form. The museum, after all, is an institution linked to the humanism Qutb rails against. The modern museum emerged in the eighteenth century in conjunction with the rise of the nation-state and the social and political upheavals of the European Enlightenment. Since then, museums have played a central role in cultivating modern mores. According to philosopher Raymond Geuss, museums have been particularly valuable for fostering "a certain kind of secular, cosmopolitan enlightenment, a cultivation of the imagination, and of the faculty of judgment."[20] In her book *Civilizing Rituals*, art historian Carol Duncan likewise describes museums as quintessentially modern sites for "publicly represent[ing] beliefs about the order of the world, its past and present, and the individual's place within it."[21] Al-Farabi might have called them prophetic institutions. "To control a museum," Duncan continues, "means precisely to control the representation of a community and its highest values and truths."

Since the beginning of their rediscovery in the vicinity of Mosul in the 1840s, ancient Mesopotamian sculptures have been incorporated into museum collections throughout the world—and so into the work those museums do. Though the famed lion hunt scenes from Nineveh no longer arouse allegiance to the Assyrian king Ashurbanipal, they have never been politically impotent while on display in the British Museum. In the next chapter, I consider the scope of meanings that museums have bestowed on ancient Mesopotamian objects over the past century and a half. Turning attention from the objects that ISIS designated as idols worthy of destruction to the stage on which that destruction took place, I ask, What is significant about the museum as the site of the Islamic State's video of destruction?

2
Museums

AS SOON AS THE notorious video was released, the blogosphere flooded with calls to action to protect antiquities from the locals—rehashing old imperial tropes about barbarism and civilization. Some argued that teams should be sent into Iraq, like the "Monuments Men" sent to World War II Europe, to rescue the cultural property that remained. "Now that Islamist madmen are on the loose across great swathes of the Middle East," Hudson Institute fellow Ann Marlowe wrote in the *Daily Beast*, "we have reason to value the cultural imperialism of years past. It was rationalized, then, as saving treasures from barbarians. Whatever the truth of the matter in those days, there is no doubt now that the barbarians are back with a vengeance."[1] In a lighter vein, cartoonist Patrick Chappatte depicted two jihadists leaving the Mosul Museum—one saying, "My first time in a museum. This was awesome!" (figure 4).

The day the video appeared, the director general of UNESCO, Irina Bokova, condemned the event as "a deliberate attack against

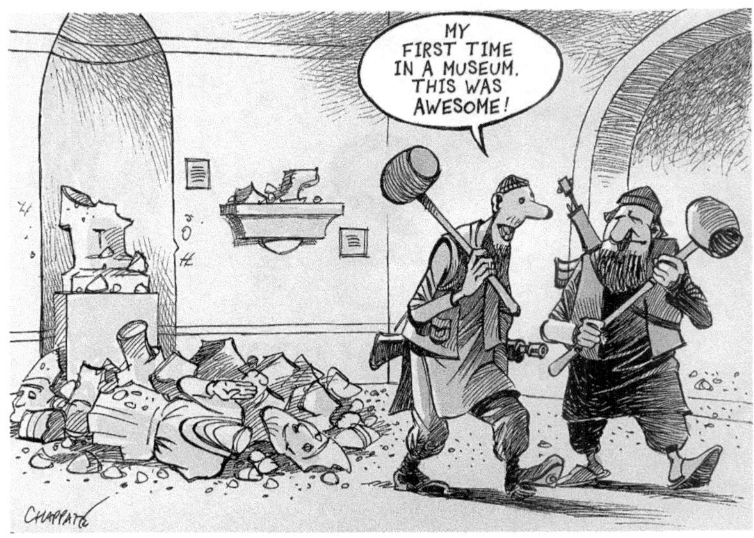

4. Patrick Chappatte, "Mosul Museum Devastated." February 28, 2015.

Iraq's millennial history and culture."[2] She called the destruction "a war crime" and insisted that "there is absolutely no political or religious justification for the destruction of humanity's cultural heritage."[3] Other cultural institutions followed with statements in short order: "Speaking with great sadness on behalf of the Metropolitan, a museum whose collection proudly protects and displays the arts of ancient and Islamic Mesopotamia," Metropolitan Museum of Art director Thomas P. Campbell wrote in a press release, "we strongly condemn this act of catastrophic destruction to one of the most important museums in the Middle East." The "mindless attack on great art, on history, and on human understanding," he asserted, was "a tragic assault not only on the Mosul Museum, but on our universal commitment to use art to unite people and promote human understanding."[4] The Oriental Institute at the University of Chicago called the destruction "deliberate vandalism" that constituted "a moral and cultural outrage."[5] The European Association of Archaeologists condemned the "cultural arrogance facing the world's cultural heritage."[6] Cairo's al-Azhar, Sunni Islam's most prestigious university, issued a similar statement. "The destruction of cultural heritage is forbidden in Islam and rejected in total," declared Grand Imam Ahmed el-Tayeb. "By claiming they are idols, Daesh [another name for ISIS] is committing a major crime against the whole world."[7]

Notice the conflicting language. Where ISIS spoke of the need to cleanse the world of idols, their critics refer to a moral and legal imperative to protect cultural heritage. Though each side points to the same material objects, what they see is different. What is at stake in the difference between idols and heritage?

We have seen how Ibrahim's campaign to rid the world of idols expressed a longing to free human life from a dependence on images. Only once human-made images are eradicated, Ibrahim surmised, can mankind genuinely serve God, whose rule requires a regime without images. But the purity of Ibrahim's imagined regime is also the mark of its impossibility. Because politics is untenable without images, the repudiation of images as idols is tantamount to the rejection of politics itself. Those who see idols long for a world beyond politics.

What about heritage? As the inheritance of a people, heritage would seem to be a fundamentally political category. Abbé Grégoire (1750–1831), the French revolutionary who coined the term "vandalism" in an effort to dampen the iconoclastic fury that had overtaken France during the Revolution, made the protection of cultural heritage the foundation of his political project. National sovereignty, the Abbé thought, is protected not only by the tips of bayonets but also by the preservation of patrimony. He promoted this view by inverting the prophetic parodies of idolatry in the Bible.

For example, Jeremiah inveighed, "Every human is too stupid to know, every smith is shamed by the idol, for the molten image is a lie, and there is no spirit in them" (10:14). By contrast, in the Abbé's *Second Report on Vandalism* (August 1794), he declared before the National Convention, "The ignorant see only a piece of crafted stone; let us show them that this piece of marble breathes, that this canvas is alive, and that this book is an arsenal with which to defend their rights."[8] In other words, iconoclasm, *not idolatry*, is the quintessential crime of ignorance. The 1793 law forbidding vandalism required that all objects of artistic, historical, or educational value be "taken to the nearest museum." Not by chance, most of those museums were repurposed local churches—or, in the case of the Louvre, a royal palace. The new storehouses of heritage were meant to replace the twin pillars of the old regime: the church and the monarchy. Museums, and the heritage they housed, would serve an emphatically political purpose.

And yet, when the European Association of Archaeologists lambasted the Islamic State for cultural arrogance, it stressed that antiquities "in no way can be considered a component of ideologically active conflicts." The ancient Mesopotamian objects housed in the Mosul Museum, in their view, are not images that help one political entity define itself against others but manifestations of civilization in its struggle against barbarism. That these objects belong to a region commonly called the "cradle of civilization" serves to underscore this point.

Though Abbé Grégoire was motivated by a concern for the French nation, his "vandalism" rhetoric prompted a framing of heritage preservation as an issue that transcends politics. Derived from the Vandals—one of the Germanic tribes that sacked and looted the Roman empire—the term connotes barbarian hoards threatening civilized life. Just as civilization supposedly stands above political divisions, barbarism is something that threatens from below. The conflict between civilization and barbarism is fundamentally different from a war between political enemies. Protecting heritage springs from a principle supposedly purer than politics: universal humanity.

The Spanish philosopher José Ortega y Gasset relates a relevant story about Victor Hugo:

> For the celebration of Victor Hugo's jubilee a grand reception was organized at the Élysée Palace to which representatives of every nation came to pay their homage. The great poet took his place in the reception hall in a solemn statuesque pose, elbow resting on the marble of a chimney. One after another the nations' delegates came forward from the crowd and presented their homage to the Master. An usher announced them in stentorian voice: "The gentleman representing England," he proclaimed, and Victor Hugo, his eyes in ecstasy, his voice shot through with dramatic tremolos, replied: "England! Ah, Shakespeare!" The usher went on: "The gentleman representing Spain"; Victor Hugo, in the same vein: "Spain! Ah, Cervantes!" "The gentleman representing Germany"; "Germany! Ah, Goethe!" But a short man stepped forward, clumsy, chubby, of rustic bearing, and the usher announced with flair: "The gentleman representing Mesopotamia." Then Victor Hugo, who until that moment had remained impassible and sure of himself, appeared troubled. His suddenly anxious pupils cast a broad look around that seemed to embrace the universe, searching in vain for something out there. But it soon became clear to the spectators that he had found it and that he once again mastered the situation. And with the same pathetic accent, the same conviction, he answered the pudgy representative with these words: "Mesopotamia! Ah, Humanity!"[9]

Hugo's reaction is emblematic of a broader tendency, since at least the mid-nineteenth century, to associate Mesopotamia with the idea of universal humanity. As the supposed birthplace of civilization, Mesopotamia has come to symbolize what all human beings share. Because the civilization of ancient Mesopotamia stands at the dawn of human history, the unity of civilization is thought to predate—and so take precedence over—political divisions. This is the myth of the Tower of Babel transposed into a modern liberal key. "In the idea of world history," writes Hannah Arendt, "the multiplicity of men is melted into *one* human individual, which is then also called humanity."[10] Mesopotamia is the quintessential symbol of that humanity and the concomitant longing to live beyond politics. Transcending politics in the name of civilization resembles Ibrahim's aversion for political images more than one might think.

And yet one must wear special blinders for Mesopotamian images to appear as apolitical as the European Association of Archaeologists wants them to be. Consider an image that circulated on social media right after the sacking of the Mosul Museum (figure 5). It shows an arrow-pierced lion from Ashurbanipal's palace in Nineveh captioned with the phrases "Stop the genocide of Assyria's civilization" and "I stand with Assyria." Most people who shared or "liked" the image on Facebook probably thought they were performing a political act in support of enlightened cosmopolitanism. Few would have recognized "Stand with Assyria" as a hashtag for the modern Assyrian nationalist movement, whose militia has battled not only ISIS but also Kurdish peshmerga forces and other groups. Does advocating the preservation of Assyrian antiquities mean one is taking sides in an obscure conflict in the Middle East, or endorsing nationalism over Enlightenment cosmopolitanism? Claiming that the images constituting heritage are apolitical is a facile way to sidestep such questions and avoid facing the implications of one's own commitments. It is no less naïve to think these images are free of politics than it was for Ibrahim to think politics could exist without images.

The suffering Assyrian lion offers but one example of the complicated ways ancient Near Eastern objects have been entangled

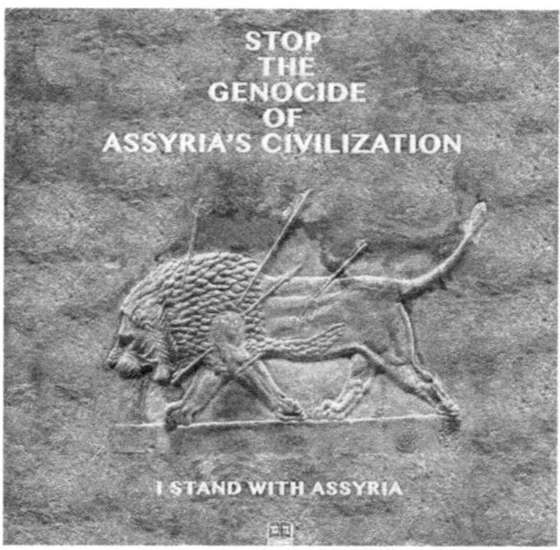

5. "Stop the Genocide of Assyria's Civilization." Meme circulated online, March 2015.

in modern politics since their rediscovery in the mid-nineteenth century. In her response to the ISIS video, UNESCO's Irina Bokova referred to the objects being destroyed sometimes as Iraq's cultural heritage and sometimes as humanity's. Her statements echo an ambivalence that has accompanied ancient Near Eastern objects for as long as they have found homes in modern museums. Understanding the origins of that ambivalence can shed light on the meaning and fate of Mesopotamian images in our own day.

Museums are far from neutral spaces providing unmediated access to the objects in their collections. The objects are accompanied by narratives that give them meaning—narratives that encourage audiences to subscribe to particular visions of the world. The dream of unmediated access is as deceptive in a museum as it is illusory in political life. Replacing the language of idolatry with the language of heritage brings us no closer to unmediated truth than did Ibrahim's acts of iconoclasm. Is it so clear-cut that museums are bastions of civilization, protecting our common heritage from destruction at the hands of barbarians? Is the value of antiquities self-evident, as if the narratives museums spin around objects were written unambiguously on their surface? Instead of blindly accepting the view that antiquities constitute a universal heritage whose destruction is barbaric, we ought to attune ourselves to how museums have cultivated this attitude and seek out what it keeps hidden from view.

●

Near Eastern antiquities have enthralled viewers from the day archaeologists began to rediscover them. As they have passed through the world's museums, they have become laden with many meanings.

The modern story begins in 1842, when the French consul in Mosul, Paul-Émile Botta (1802–1870), set out to discover the ancient city of Nineveh. The last Assyrian capital had long been known to Westerners from the Bible and Greco-Roman historians. Medieval Christians often conflated its legendary founder, Ninus, with the biblical Nimrod. Fascination with the Assyrian empire had intensified in the 1820s—as attested by Lord Byron's 1821 reading-drama *The Tragedy of Sardanapalus* (as Ashurbanipal was known from classical sources) and Eugène Delacroix's *The Death of Sardanapalus*, first displayed at the Salon of 1827–1828 (figure 6). In Delacroix's painting, the Assyrian king lounges nonchalantly as his empire burns; it is a scathing indictment of absolutist despotism, not least that of France's restored king Charles X. Botta moved in the same Parisian circles as Delacroix before being appointed consul under Charles X's successor, the "bourgeois king" Louis-Philippe. Originally trained as a naturalist, he undertook the search for Nineveh in the spirit of scientific advancement that defined his liberal age. "As usual, [the French government] has nobly encouraged these researches so important to history and so useful for a knowledge

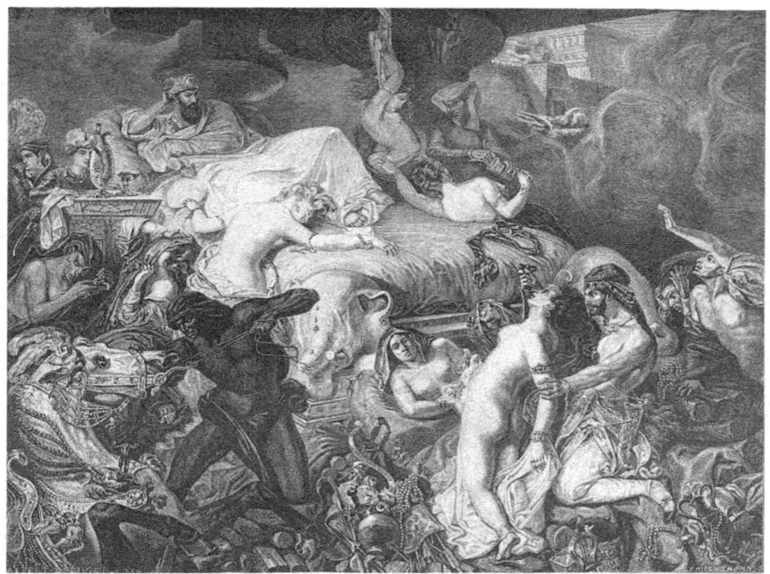

6. Engraving by Emile Thomas (French, 1841–1907) after Eugène Delacroix's *The Death of Sardanapalus* (1827, Louvre). *Le Monde Illustré*, May 16, 1874. Metropolitan Museum of Art.

of ancient art among the bygone nations of Mesopotamia," Botta wrote to Jules Mohl, his backer at the Société asiatique. "May such liberal intentions not be frustrated by ignorance and barbarism."[11]

Botta began his search on the large tell on the east bank of the Tigris River directly across from Mosul, by the village of Kuyunjik. Before long he moved his men sixteen kilometers northwest to a more promising mound near the village of Khorsabad. Within three days, his foreman, Naaman Ibn Naush, announced that the team had discovered decorated stone slabs and cuneiform inscriptions. The Ottoman sultan in Istanbul authorized a full excavation. Together with Eugène Flandin—an artist dispatched to assist in recording the finds—and a team of local workmen, Botta brought

Sargon II's palace of Dur-Sharrukin to light for the first time in over two thousand years.

Cuneiform script had not yet been deciphered, so Botta couldn't know precisely what he had unearthed; he vaguely informed his supporters in Paris that he had "discover[ed] sculptures which may be assumed to belong to the time when Nineveh was still flourishing."[12] The first shipment of Assyrian reliefs arrived at the Louvre in January 1847. Botta remained in Mosul and continued excavating at Khorsabad until he was transferred to a lower position in Jerusalem in reprisal for his royalist stance during the 1848 revolution. (The French consulate in Jerusalem is today located on a street bearing his name.) The novelist Gustave Flaubert, who visited Botta in Jerusalem, described him as "a ruined man, a man of ruins, in the city of ruins."[13] Botta died, forgotten, in 1870.

Austen Henry Layard (1817–1894), one of the great archaeologists of the Victorian age, first met Botta when he stopped in Mosul on his way to Istanbul in June 1842—nine months before the Frenchman began excavating at Khorsabad. The twenty-five-year-old British adventurer in Bakhtiyari tribal attire had arrived from Baghdad after two years traveling throughout Persia. Layard had been in Mosul once before, in 1840, and glimpsed the ruins known locally as Nimrud, named after Ibrahim's legendary antagonist. "As the sun went down," he recounted in his *Autobiography*,

> I saw for the first time the great conical mound of Nimrud rising against the clear evening sky. It was on the opposite side of the river and not very distant, and the impression that it made upon me was one never to be forgotten. After my visit to Kuyunjik and Nebbi Yunus, opposite Mosul, and the distant view of Nimrud, my thought ran constantly upon the possibility of thoroughly exploring with the spade those great ruins.[14]

Layard traveled to Kuyunjik with Botta, where the two men discussed their aspirations to uncover the remains of ancient Assyria. Three days later, Layard was on his way to Istanbul—where he would establish himself in the service of the British ambassador to the Ottoman empire, Sir Stratford Canning. When Botta's finds at Khorsabad became public, Layard convinced Canning to support an expedition of his own to Nimrud. In the guise of "a traveler, fond of antiquities, of picturesque scenery, and of the manners peculiar to Asia," Layard returned to Mosul in October 1845 and began digging at Nimrud.[15]

The first relief sculptures emerged the following month. Soon thereafter, Canning acquired a *firman* from the Ottoman grand vizier permitting Layard to continue his research and to send "antique stones on which there are figures and inscriptions" back to England.[16] The first twelve cases set sail from Basra in the fall of 1846, were put on view by the Asiatic Society of Bombay that December, and finally arrived at the British Museum in June 1847. "They have created great interest," the museum's secretary of the trustees wrote to Layard, "and all who have examined them appear to be much gratified."[17] Layard would achieve celebrity and, eventually, a seat in parliament. His book *Nineveh and Its Remains*—part archaeological report, part adventure story—was a national bestseller.

The advancement of science (for Botta) and the thrill of discovery (for Layard) were inseparable from nineteenth-century imperial politics. Both men were commissioned by their governments to advance, respectively, French and British interests in the Ottoman empire. Their backers in Paris and London saw the expeditions as opportunities to enhance national prestige. Jules Mohl, president of the Société asiatique, expressed the official French attitude with his promise that "everything admitting of removal will be sent to

France, and there form an Assyrian museum, unique throughout the world."[18] The frontispiece to *Nineveh and Its Remains* emphasized the immense effort required to haul away a colossal *lamassu* (figure 7). This image of British technical achievement echoes the Assyrian kings' own display of imperial power—as Layard himself would discover while excavating Sennacherib's palace at Nineveh just months after his bestseller was published (figure 8).

The Louvre's Assyrian galleries opened to the public in the presence of King Louis-Philippe on May 1, 1847. "Whether Nebuchadnezzar, Sardanapalus, or Ninus (for we aren't sure who he is), the Assyrian monarch has set foot on the banks of the Seine," the newspaper *L'Illustration* announced. Alluding to the Louvre's ambiguous status as both museum and palace, it observed, "He was destined for a new home worthier of him—the palace of our kings."[19] Louis-Philippe's government also bankrolled Botta and Flandin's magisterial five-volume *Monument de Ninive*—spending almost three times more on the publication than on the entire course of excavations. As the title suggests, the book served not merely as

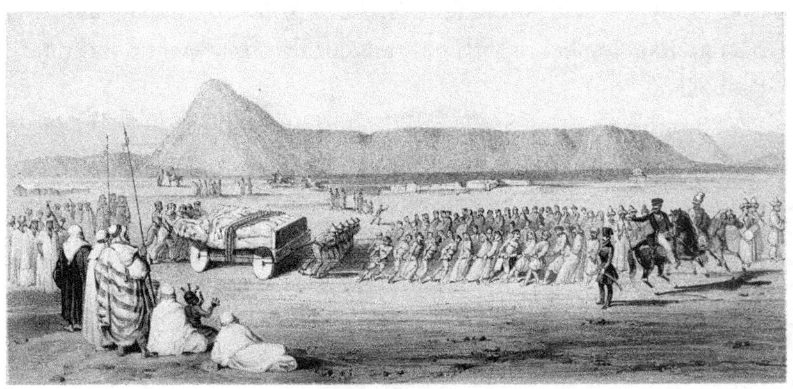

7. "Procession of the Bull beneath the Mound of Nimroud." Austen Henry Layard, *Niniveh and Its Remains*, 1849.

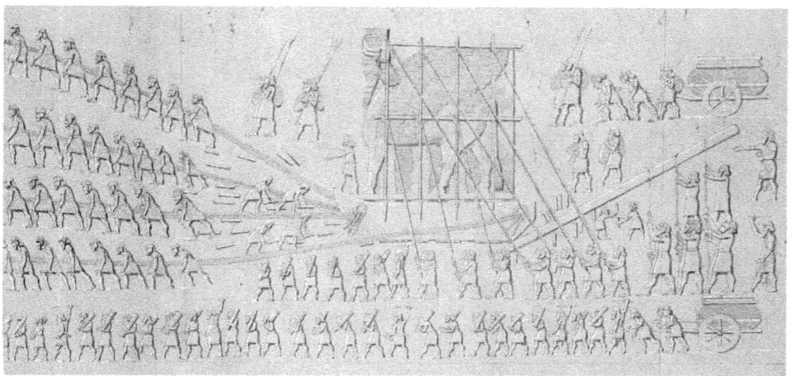

8. Drawing by F. C. Cooper of an Assyrian relief depicting the transport of a *lamassu*, Court VI of the Southwest Palace at Nineveh, 1849. British Museum.

a document of ancient royal monuments but as a monument to the current king of France.

In this contest for national prestige, the British would not be outdone. In 1846 Layard's promoter, Stratford Canning, assured the British prime minister that thanks to the discoveries at Nimrud the British Museum "will beat the Louvre hollow."[20] Installed the following year, the Assyrian works proved an immediate success with the English public. An etching of the museum's Nineveh Room published in the *Illustrated London News* depicts the newly acquired objects in a gallery peopled with respectably dressed men and women; in the foreground, two men inspect a column base, while a mother explains a work to her two children (figure 9). In his study of the nineteenth-century reception of Assyrian antiquities, art historian Frederick Bohrer argues that the engraving offered the magazine's wide readership an image of their ideal selves—dignified citizens of an empire that affords them the opportunity to contemplate a past configured to glorify their own present. It set museumgoing—not unlike churchgoing in the past—as a marker of civilized life to which all self-respecting citizens might aspire.

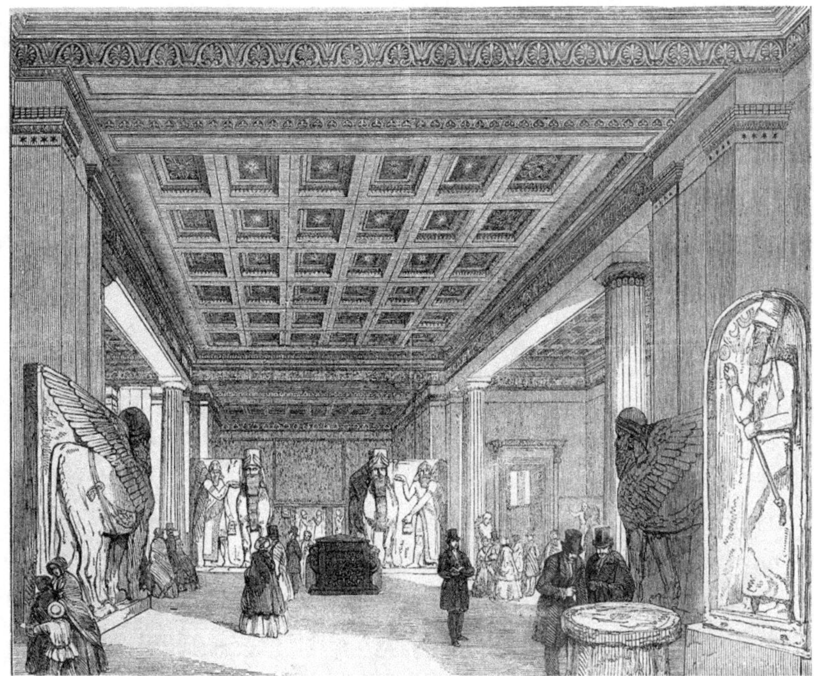

9. The Nineveh Room in the British Museum. *Illustrated London News*, 1853.

Visiting the museum and practicing the behavior modeled in the engraving reinforced commitment to the empire that made civilized life possible. But such visits were not essential—the museum could assert its power even if one only visited it in one's imagination.

"Look at these stupid foreigners!" the Ottoman sultan Abdul Hamid II (r. 1876–1909) reportedly remarked. "I pacify them with broken stones."[21] Though the Ottomans did take advantage of the European craving for ancient artifacts to advance their own state interests, the quotation taxes credulity. It was during Abdul Hamid's reign, at any rate, that the Ottoman policy of preserving and displaying antiquities unearthed within the realm came of age. In 1869 the Sublime Porte, the empire's central government, approved the idea of a "perfect museum" since "it is not appropriate that the museums in Europe should be filled and decorated mostly with antiquities taken from here, while we do not even have a museum."[22] The Ottoman government commissioned archaeology enthusiast and Paris-trained painter Osman Hamdi Bey (1842–1910) to undertake excavations at Mount Nemrud, a mountain in southeastern Turkey said to be Nimrud's burial site (figure 10). Pleased with the results, Abdul Hamid II ordered that a building be constructed to house the finds.

Under the direction of Osman Hamdi, the Imperial Museum in Istanbul provided a space where the diversity of the Ottoman empire could appear as a unity. The display of antiquities not only sought to rival the Louvre and the British Museum in prestige

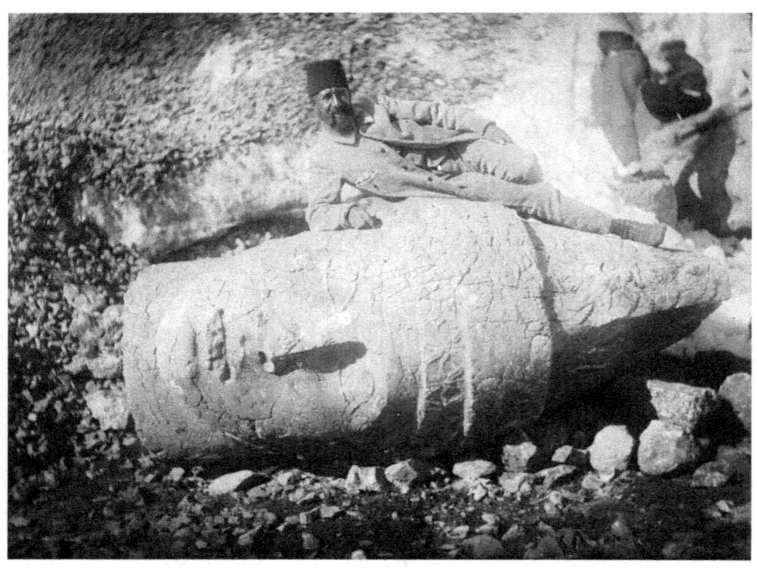

10. Osman Hamdi Bey posing with the head of Antiochos on the western terrace of Mount Nemrud, 1883. Istanbul Archaeological Museums, Photographic Archives, 11190.

but asserted imperial coherence in the face of European incursions on Ottoman territory. This imperial message was carefully crafted through photographs. Included in Abdul Hamid's exhaustive photo albums documenting the realm were images that show artifacts being carefully removed and transported using the latest technology—old and new working together to create a museum to promote the Ottoman state. The sultan presented sumptuous sets of these albums to the British Museum and the US Library of Congress in 1894. One could tour the imperial districts along the Tigris and Euphrates Rivers while sitting by the Thames or Potomac.

•

Imperial interests intertwined with aesthetic debates. When the first sculptures arrived in London, a parliamentary commission asked Sir Richard Westmacott, a professor of sculpture at the British Royal Academy and a trustee of the British Museum, for his opinion of the newly acquired treasures from the ancient Near East. "It is very bad art," he replied.[23]

Layard disagreed. In 1845 he published an article praising the artistic worth of the objects Botta had discovered at Khorsabad. "To those who have been accustomed to look upon the Greeks as the true perfecters and the only masters of the imitative arts, [these finds] will furnish new matter for inquiry and reflection," he remarks. "They are immeasurably superior to the stiff and ill-proportioned figures of the monuments of the Pharaohs. . . . In fact, the great gulf which separates barbarian from civilized art has been passed."[24] Even in praising Mesopotamian artistic achievement, Layard hews closely to the canons of good taste. He does not challenge the idea of a gulf separating barbarism from civilization; he just shifts the dividing line. To further assimilate Assyrian sculpture to nineteenth-century aesthetic standards, some relief panels were cut down to produce "portrait" heads and other recognizable artistic configurations.

Whether "bad art" or not, the newly acquired Mesopotamian objects captivated the imaginations of modern artists. French symbolist painter Gustave Moreau filled a sketchbook with exquisite studies based on the Louvre's Khorsabad reliefs (figure 11), and the sculptor Jacob Epstein based Oscar Wilde's tomb in Père-Lachaise on the Assyrian winged bulls that dazzled audiences in Paris and London (figure 12). Years later, after the Louvre added Sumerian sculpture to its collection, the Swiss artist Alberto Giacometti

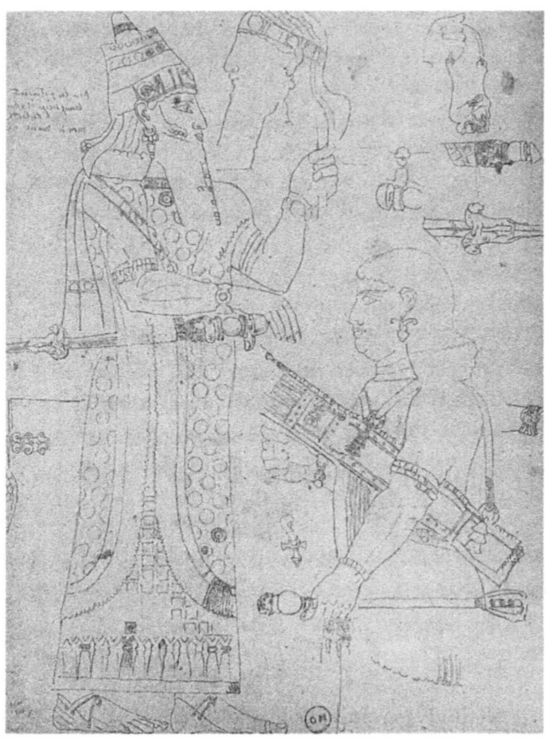

11. Pencil sketch of Assyrian figures by Gustave Moreau, ca. 1860–1870. Musée Gustave Moreau, Paris.

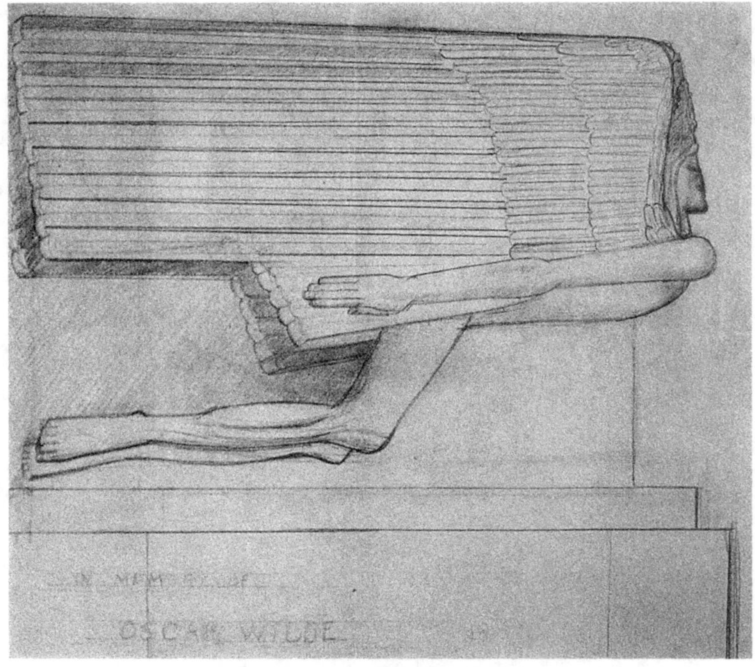

12. Jacob Epstein's study for the tomb of Oscar Wilde, ca. 1908. Courtesy New Art Gallery Walsall, UK.

transformed stately diorite figurines of ancient kings into whimsical line compositions using blue ballpoint pen. In America, film pioneer D. W. Griffith rebuilt ancient Babylon on Hollywood's Sunset Boulevard for his ruinously expensive epic *Intolerance* (1916). The set featured both relatively accurate *lamassu* sculptures and totally inappropriate sculptures of rearing elephants. Griffith reportedly complained that the studio builders deviated from the research on Babylonian art and architecture he had compiled in a scrapbook now housed in New York's Museum of Modern Art (figure 13).

Twenty years later, Alfred Barr (1902–1981), MoMA's first director, ensconced "Near-Eastern art" in the story of modernism, summarized in a flowchart on the cover of the catalogue for his landmark exhibition *Cubism and Abstract Art* (figure 14). The influence of Mesopotamian sculpture of the first millennium BCE appears in Barr's diagram between 1900 and 1905, a decade after that of nineteenth-century Japanese woodblock prints and just before that of "Negro sculpture" and the "machine esthetic" of contemporary industrial society. This convoluted chronology derives from a focus on form. "A work of art," Barr asserted, "is worth looking at primarily because it presents a composition or organization of color, line, light and shade."[25] Barr's formalist approach severs works of art

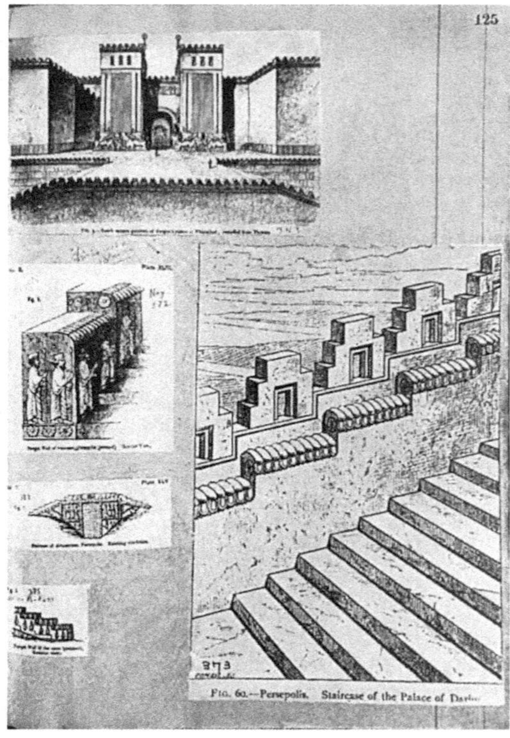

13. Page from D. W. Griffith's scrapbook for *Intolerance*, 1916. Griffith Archives, Museum of Modern Art, New York.

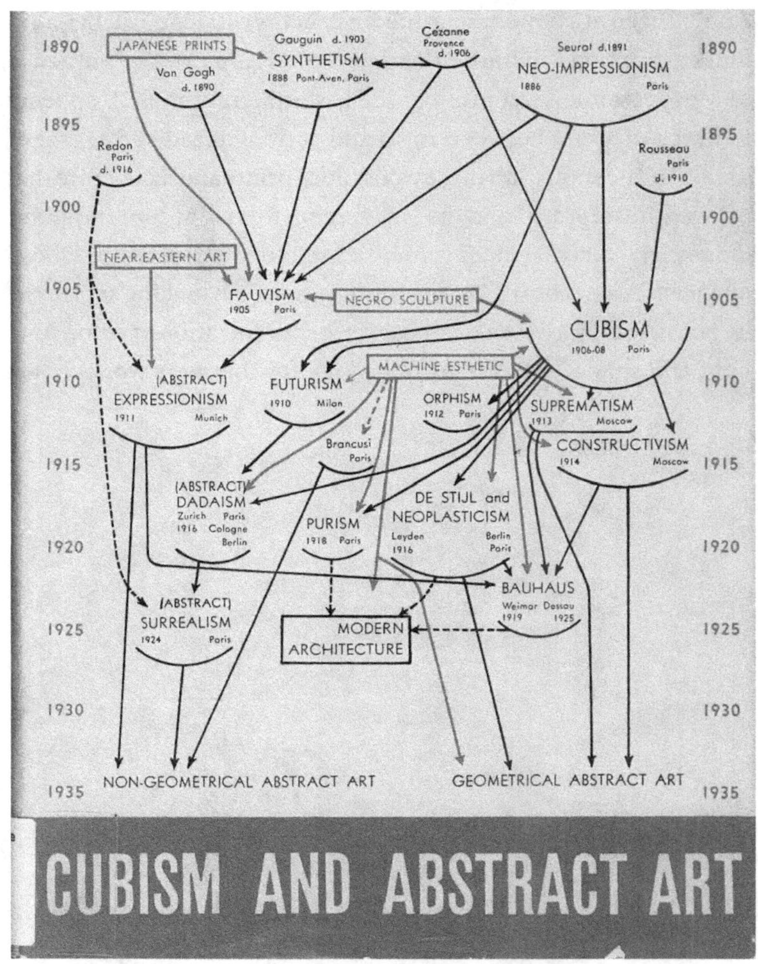

14. Alfred H. Barr Jr.'s cover design for *Cubism and Abstract Art* exhibition catalogue, 1936. Museum of Modern Art, New York.

from the political, economic, and cultural contexts of their production; what matters is how a work resolves formal problems internal to itself. As a purveyor of modernism, Barr did not so much produce new images as teach people to see all images in new ways. He held out the promise of a cosmopolitanism based on the appreciation of pure form; Near Eastern art had its part to play in bringing about this new order.

As Barr was preparing *Cubism and Abstract Art*, British sculptor Henry Moore (1898–1986) likewise affirmed the universal appeal of Near Eastern art. "For me," Moore wrote in *The Listener*, "Sumerian sculpture ranks with Early Greek, Etruscan, Ancient Mexican, Fourth and Twelfth Dynasty Egyptian, and Romanesque and Early Gothic sculpture, as the great sculpture of the world."[26] As his list implies, Moore did not organize artistic traditions into a rigid teleological framework, whether of civilization or (as Barr had) modernism; for him, great sculpture could arise wherever and whenever social conditions were ripe. "It is not necessary to know their history in order to appreciate and respond to these works of art," Moore asserts, since "once a good piece of sculpture has been produced . . . it is real and a part of life, here and now, to those sensitive and open enough to feel and perceive it." The traditions that earned a place in Moore's pantheon each communicated "a deep human element." Knowing too much about a Sumerian sculpture's temple function or the political ambitions that gave rise to an Assyrian relief could only obscure our vision of the "human element" that justifies our engagement with (and possession of) these works of art. Mesopotamian art "belongs to all of us" not because we (or our ancestors) fashioned it, but because we can all appreciate it.°

° Moore's interest in images that speak to all mankind takes on added significance in light of his friendship with Julian Huxley (1887–1975), UNESCO's first director general. On the heels of the most devastating war in human history, Huxley—in a spirit reminiscent of Nimrud's endeavor

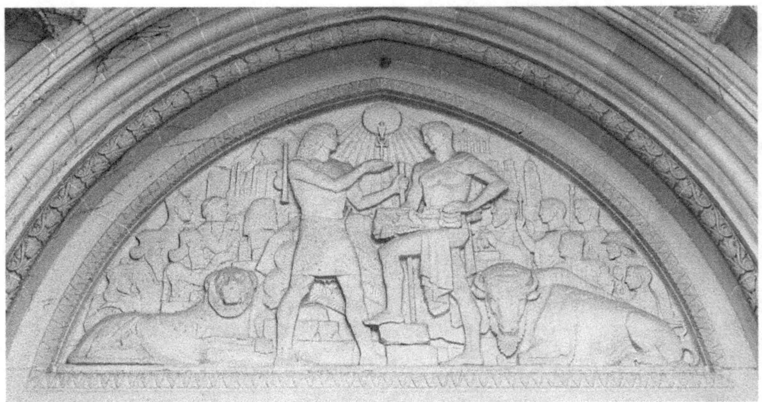

15. Tympanum over the entrance to the Oriental Institute at the University of Chicago, after a design by James Henry Breasted.

The tympanum welcoming visitors to the Oriental Institute at the University of Chicago celebrates the ancient Near East in a different mode (figure 15). At the center of the composition, designed by the institute's founder, James Henry Breasted (1865–1935), a figure holds an archaeological fragment inscribed in Egyptian hieroglyphs with the phrase "We behold thy beauty." But who is this "we"?

---

to build the Tower of Babel after the flood—imagined the United Nations Educational, Scientific and Cultural Organization as a vehicle for preventing future calamities. In his 1946 manifesto *UNESCO: Its Purpose and Its Philosophy*, Huxley argued that the only certain way to avoid future wars was to establish "some form of world political unity, whether through a single world government or otherwise." Though he admitted that UNESCO's authority over education, science, and culture was not sufficient to this task, he nevertheless envisioned the organization as contributing to "the emergence of a single world culture." The stakes were high. "Since another war would be so appalling as to set back the march of human progress by centuries," Huxley concluded, "I am convinced that the task of achieving this synthesis in time to forestall open conflict must be the overriding aim of UNESCO." In 1957, UNESCO's Committee on Architecture and Works of Art commissioned *Reclining Figure*, the largest sculpture Moore ever made, for the organization's headquarters in Paris.

The tympanum does not characterize this appreciative audience in the universal humanistic terms espoused by Moore. Instead, it situates the appreciation of beauty within a transfer of heritage from ancient East to modern West. The scene depicts a reverent youth representing the West receiving civilization from an Egyptian figure, the latter flanked by a lion and the former (in good Midwestern fashion) by a bison. Breasted clarified the symbolism in an internal memorandum from 1932. "Above the animals," he explained, "outstanding figures of the Eastern and Western civilizations are shown."[27] For the East, these include two Egyptian pharaohs, the

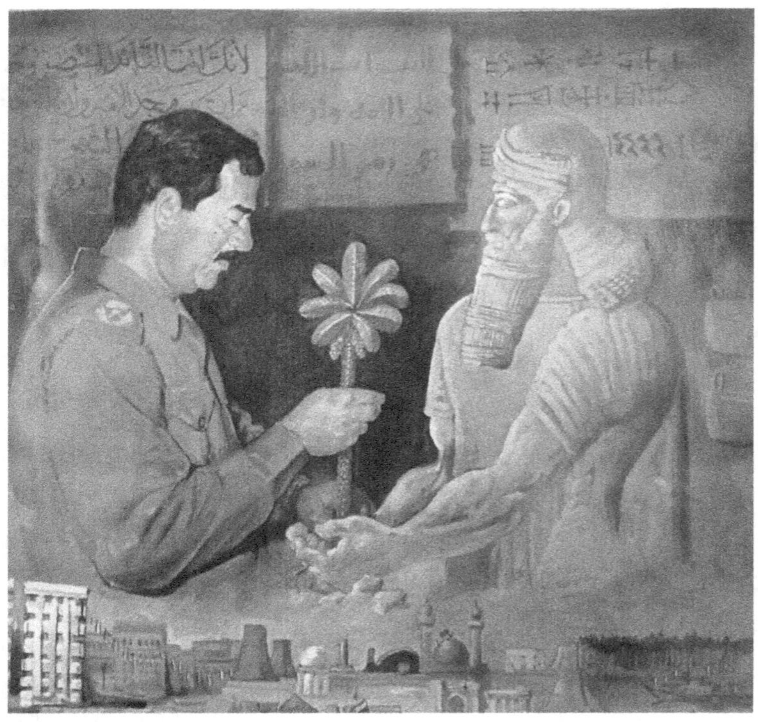

16. Saddam Hussein receiving Iraqi cultural heritage from a Mesopotamian deity. *Alif Ba*, January 8, 1968.

Babylonian king Hammurabi, the Assyrian Ashurnasirpal, and the Persian Darius. The Western figures include Herodotus, Alexander the Great, the Roman emperor Augustus, a crusader, a field archaeologist, and a museum curator examining a vase with a magnifying glass. Columns from Persepolis, a sphinx, and three pyramids represent the art and architecture of the East. The Parthenon, Notre Dame cathedral, and the Nebraska state capitol represent the West. Islam is conspicuously absent.

Like archaeologists who once commonly removed so-called late levels—that is, medieval and modern Islamic remains—without recording them to get to the ancient layers underneath, Breasted elides the Islamic Middle East as though only the West beholds antiquity's beauty today. Here Moore's universalist sentiment that art belongs to anyone sensitive enough to grasp it takes on a less sanguine hue: it becomes a criterion for supersession. The political undertones involved in beholding ancient Near Eastern beauty can't be avoided simply by declaring art apolitical. Breasted boldly avowed his stance above the Oriental Institute's entrance; visitors to the museum today must consider for themselves how the tympanum will inflect their engagement with the objects inside.

●

How have images from the ancient Near East been appropriated on their native soil? An image of Saddam Hussein published in the state-sponsored Iraqi periodical *Alif-Ba* on January 8, 1986, echoes Breasted's tympanum (figure 16). In place of the muscular Western youth accepting the civilization of the East, Saddam receives a palm sapling representing Iraqi heritage from an Assyrian figure. The movement now runs from right to left, in accord with the direction of Arabic writing. In the background, three passages celebrating Saddam as a victorious leader—in cuneiform and medieval and modern

Arabic scripts—symbolize the continuity of Iraqi literary culture. Beneath the main figures ancient ships sail down the Tigris beside palatial Islamic architecture and a modern cityscape complete with the silos of power plants. Iraq's tricolor flag not only adorns the modern apartment blocks but flies atop the medieval domes and the masts of the ancient ships. The palm sapling—in contrast to Breasted's isolated archaeological fragment—emphasizes local rootedness; it likely also embeds a visual pun on the word *nachla*, meaning "palm" in Arabic but "inheritance" in Aramaic. Several members of the Iraqi archaeological establishment—beginning with Taha Baqir and Fu'ad Sufar in the 1930s—trained at the University of Chicago. Was the Iraqi artist who created this counterimage to the Oriental Institute tympanum aware of Breasted's image? I don't know. But either way, it marks a climax in the nationalist Iraqi claim on the ancient Mesopotamian past.

It is difficult to reconstruct today what residents around Mosul in the 1840s thought about Layard's discoveries. Playing to his readership's prejudices, the Englishman depicted the local Arabs as superstitious children who could mistake the sculpted head of a *lamassu* for the specter of Nimrud himself. "I was not surprised that the Arabs had been amazed and terrified at this apparition," he writes. "This gigantic head, blanched with age, thus rising from the bowels of the earth, might well have belonged to one of those fearful beings which are described in the traditions of the country as appearing to mortals, slowly ascending from the regions below."[28] Layard, by contrast, "saw at once that the head must belong to a winged bull or lion." An illustration in *Nineveh and Its Remains* depicts the local sheikh Abd-ur-rahman cautiously inspecting the colossal head while his companion throws up his arms in reverent awe (figure 17). Other members of the tribe (and a camel) look on from a safe distance atop the trench. The book's British readers could contrast their own sophisticated appreciation of ancient

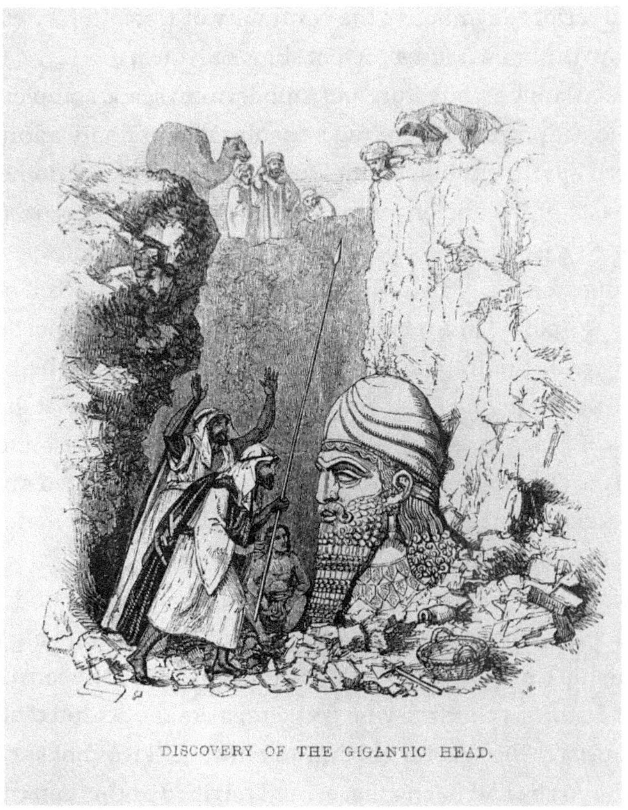

17. "Discovery of the Gigantic Head." Austen Henry Layard, *Nineveh and Its Remains*, 1849.

objects—as depicted in the *Illustrated London News* etching of the Nineveh Room (figure 9)—with the superstition of the East.

Self-serving caricature notwithstanding, Layard's account of the locals is accurate in one crucial respect: the diggers he employed most likely did not consider themselves to be unearthing their own heritage. They primarily defined themselves as products of a complicated set of overlapping allegiances to tribal chiefs, religious traditions, local pashas, and the sultan in Istanbul—not as descendants of Nimrud. Those who had claims to the land might have considered the objects lying underground to be their property—but in the impersonal sense of resources they might trade and profit from (like the oil that would soon be discovered beneath the same sands). For Layard's workers, the bond to old stones that Abbé Grégoire tried to instill among the French did not yet exist.

In the spring of 1870, Ahmed Sakir Bey (1838–1899), subgovernor of the district of Baghdad, embarked on an expedition to survey the conditions for modern steam navigation along the upper reaches of the Euphrates. His report represents an early attempt to cultivate appreciation of ancient ruins among those living in the province of Ottoman Baghdad. While navigating the Euphrates, Ahmed Sakir sent back nine letters and a telegram to be published in the official newspaper *Zevra*. The letters discussed navigational matters, observations on Bedouin agriculture, appreciation for local town planning, and descriptions of the ancient monuments that dotted the expedition's course. Resisting pressure to keep the journey on pace, Ahmed Sakir deployed teams to measure the ruins and collect pottery samples. Describing the expansive mound of Salihiyya (ancient Dura Europos), the subgovernor suggested that a proper inspection of the site would be promising since "the Franks" (i.e., European Christians) had not yet excavated there.

What warranted this extensive discussion of ancient ruins in an official provincial gazette? *Zevra*'s editor imagined a bright future for his native land. He believed that if readers recognized Iraq's ancient glory they would be motivated to restore the region's wealth and prosperity after many years of neglect. Ironically, this early attempt to inspire local interest in ancient Iraqi heritage focused on ruins that wouldn't qualify as Iraqi today. When modern borders were drawn after World War I, the ruins of Dura Europos fell on the Syrian side of Sykes-Picot's line in the sand.

At the San Remo Conference in 1920, the French and British

agreed that the three former Ottoman administrative districts of Basra, Baghdad, and Mosul would be transformed into the "State of Iraq" under British mandate. The territory contained a diverse population: Arabs and Kurds, Sunni and Shiite Muslims, considerable Christian and Jewish populations, and smaller minority groups such as Yazidis. Iraq was to be a constitutional monarchy, but given its ethnic and sectarian schisms it seemed virtually impossible to find a local candidate for king. Eventually, the British found their solution in Faysal bin Hussein (1885–1933), third son of Hussein bin Ali, the Hashemite sharif of Mecca who had proclaimed the Arab Revolt against the Ottoman Turks in 1906. Deposed from his brief reign as king of Syria by the French in 1920, Faysal became available to the British. His pedigree, the British believed, would make him acceptable to the citizens of the new Iraq; his pragmatic, pliable character made him acceptable to the British. In his coronation speech, Faysal reminded the "beloved people of Iraq" that "this country was formerly the cradle of civilization." He prayed for "success in elevating the state of this dear country and this noble nation so that its ancient glory may be restored."[29]

"Faysal was very eager to know about ancient monuments," wrote Gertrude Bell (1868–1926) to her father a month before the coronation.[30] The first woman to earn a first-class degree in modern history from Oxford, Bell was an English writer, traveler, archaeologist, and spy who had been working for the British administration in Baghdad as Oriental secretary since 1917. When Faysal arrived from Syria, she became one of his chief advisers and confidantes. Recognizing that Mesopotamian artifacts could help define an Iraqi national identity, the king appointed Bell director of antiquities. He tasked her with formulating an antiquities law and endorsed her ambition to found a National Museum in Baghdad. In 1924 a law was passed that ensured half of all excavated objects would remain in the country. The museum opened two years later.

Not everyone in the new Iraqi administration agreed with the museum's underlying goals. The prominent Arab nationalist Sati al-Husri (1882–1968) followed his childhood friend Faysal to Iraq in 1920. As Iraq's first director general of education, he designed an educational program that would strengthen the idea of an Arab nation that spanned the entire region, of which the "Arabness of Iraq" was only a part. Arab history, according to al-Husri, began with the Arab kingdoms of the Yemen, developed under the Ghasam and Nabatean states, and flowered in the Golden Age of Islamic-Arab civilization. Arabs, including those living in Iraq, were taught to emulate warriors like the Prophet's companion Khalid ibn al-Walid and philosophers like al-Ma'arri, not Sumerian kings. As his fellow Iraqi pan-Arabist ʿAbd al-Rahman al-Bazzaz (1913–1973) would later put it, "An Iraqi must not forget . . . that he is not of the seed of the Babylonians, nor of the Assyrians; he is an Arab, in every sense of Arabism."[31]

In this view, Mesopotamian antiquities were more liabilities than inherited treasures. A national consciousness formed around a Mesopotamian past that not all Arabs could embrace would be at odds with the Arab cause. It comes as no surprise that al-Husri and Bell did not see eye to eye. When the director general of education first visited the museum Bell had designed, he was shocked by how little attention it gave to Iraq's Islamic heritage; he chose not to include museum trips in the Iraqi school curriculum. Years later, after both Bell and Faysal were dead, al-Husri was appointed to Bell's former post as Iraq's director of antiquities. Under his leadership, practically all of the department's funds and energies were redirected toward restoring Islamic monuments and establishing the Museum of Arab Antiquities in 1937.

"For good painting in the Arab World you have to go to Baghdad."[32] So declared the catalogue of a traveling exhibition of contemporary Iraqi art in 1965. Modern art had by then been thriving in Iraq for over a decade, stimulated by Baghdad's free and tolerant cultural climate. Foremost among Iraqi artists of the day was Jawad Salim (1920–1961). While a student at London's Slade School of Art, where he studied with Henry Moore, Salim spent long hours with the ancient Mesopotamian sculpture in the British Museum. He acquired a keen sense of how Western cultural and political imperialism worked in his native country and sought artistic means to resist their corrosive effect by giving sharper definition to Iraq's emerging national aspirations.

"He set out to prove that [Iraqis] could be proud of their ancient heritage and did not need to feel inferior to anyone," Salim's widow and fellow artist Lorna Salim recalled. "His aim was to create an artistic language unique to Iraq, built on the great art of its past civilizations—Sumer, Babylon, Assyria and of course Islam, but a language of the 20th century."[33] As director of the sculpture section of Baghdad's Institute of Fine Arts and cofounder of the Baghdad Modern Art Group, Salim worked to impart this vision to others: an Iraqi art that subsumed religious, ethnic, and sectarian impulses under a single secular national identity. Many of the young painters and sculptors of the Baghdad Modern Art Group—whose manifesto called on artists to mine the riches of a tradition that reached from Sumerian and Assyrian monuments to the magnificent miniatures of Baghdadi painter Yihya al-Wasiti—also served as conservators for the Antiquities Department and National Museum.

Iraqi resentment of Western imperialism culminated in the 1958 revolution that ousted the British-backed Hashemite monarchy and installed a socialist government under the leadership of General Abdul Karim Qasim (1914–1963). From July 1958 until his overthrow in a Baʿathist coup in February 1963, Prime Minister Qasim steered Iraq away from the pan-Arabism that had oriented men like al-Husri. Qasim introduced new national symbols with strong ancient Mesopotamian connotations—an emblem with the Akkadian sun

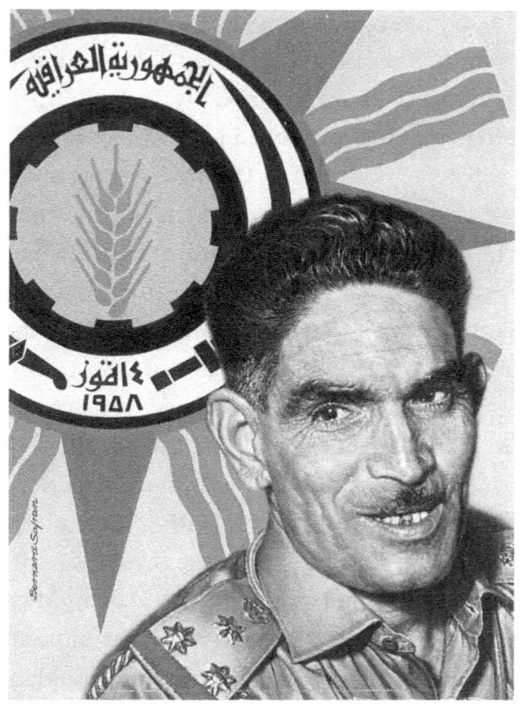

18. Bernard Safran, *Abdul Karim Kassem*, 1959. Tempera on board, 59 × 46.3 cm. National Portrait Gallery, Smithsonian Institution; gift of *Time* magazine. © Estate of Bernard Safran.

(an eight-pointed star with stylized waves between its points; figure 18) and a new Iraqi flag featuring the (also eight-pointed) star of Ishtar. Evocations of ancient Mesopotamia dominated celebrations marking the first Revolution Day. Floats depicted the invention of writing, Hammurabi's code of law, and the Ziggurat of Ur. A large portrait of Qasim—flanked by the symbols of the Sumerian god of spring, Dumuzi—led the procession. Playing on the meaning of the god's name, an inscription in cuneiform read, "Dumu-zi Ab-du-ul Ka-ri-im"—that is, "the good son Abdul Karim [Qasim]."[34]

To bolster its image, the new regime commissioned Jawad Salim to create a monument celebrating the 1958 revolution. Salim credited ancient Mesopotamian art—notably, the suffering lions of the Nineveh reliefs that had provoked his compassion in the British Museum—with teaching him how to introduce tragedy, and his own artistic voice, into grandiose depictions of state power. "The artist has always been free to express himself, even amid the state art of Assyria," he told his friend, the poet and critic Jabra Ibrahim Jabra. "The true artist speaks through the drama of the wounded beast."[35] Salim's Monument of Freedom was unveiled in Tahrir Square, in the center of Baghdad, on the second anniversary of the revolution (figure 19). Its large bronze figures, set against a raised wall designed by the architect Rifat Chadirji, make a double allusion, both to the monumental relief compositions that adorned the palaces of ancient Assyrian kings and to the revolutionary aims of the newly invigorated nation. Harnessing the ancient Mesopotamian past to envision a postcolonial future, the monument expressed "Iraq's desire for liberty since the dawn of history and the sacrifices made for its realization."[36] Though there was talk of tearing it down after the 2003 American-led invasion, the monument still stands in Baghdad as a testament to that still-unfulfilled desire.

The rise of Saddam Hussein (1937–2006) introduced a new twist to the story of Iraq's engagement with Mesopotamian antiquity. His Baʿath party was ideologically pan-Arab; the constitution it established for Iraq stated that the country's principal aim was "to achieve the United Arab State."[37] But in practice Saddam tended toward a policy reminiscent of Stalin's "socialism in one country." The traditional Baʿathist approach regarded each of the Arab states as equally illegitimate, because they were arbitrarily created by Western imperialism. In contrast, Saddam cultivated the notion of an Iraq destined by its illustrious history to lead the Arab world.

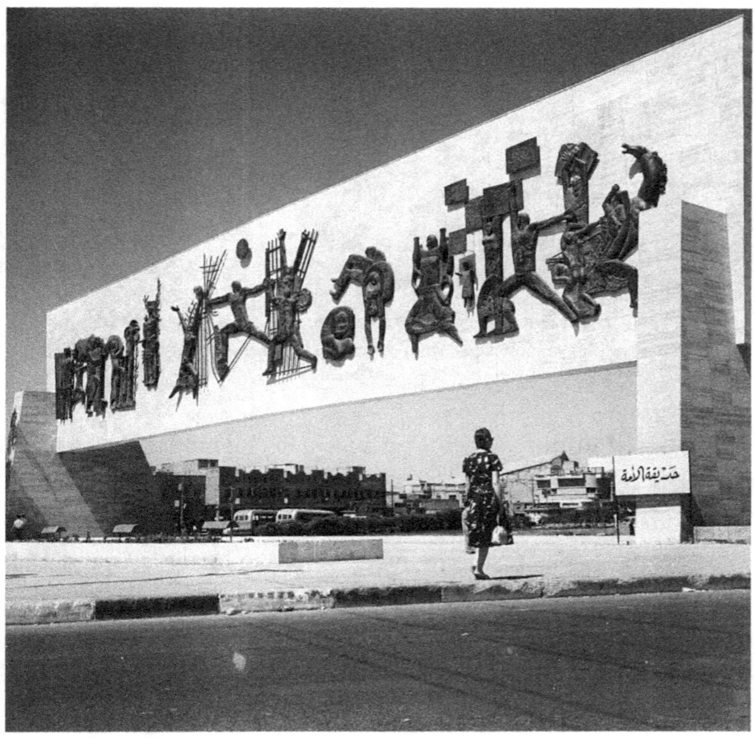

19. Latif Al-Ani, Jawad Salim's Monument of Freedom in Tahrir Square, Baghdad, Iraq, 1960s. Print from gelatin silver negative. Latif Al-Ani collection. Courtesy of the Arab Image Foundation.

Like Faysal and Qasim before him, only with greater extravagance, Saddam mined Iraq's ancient past for the sake of present political gain. Baʿathist image-makers churned out scores of images depicting Saddam in one ancient guise or another: Saddam receiving a palm sapling from a Babylonian god (figure 16); a double portrait with Babylonian king Nebuchadnezzar II on a coin commemorating the Babylon International Festival; a lion hunt scene based on the palace reliefs from Nimrud (figure 20). The Iraqi dictator also

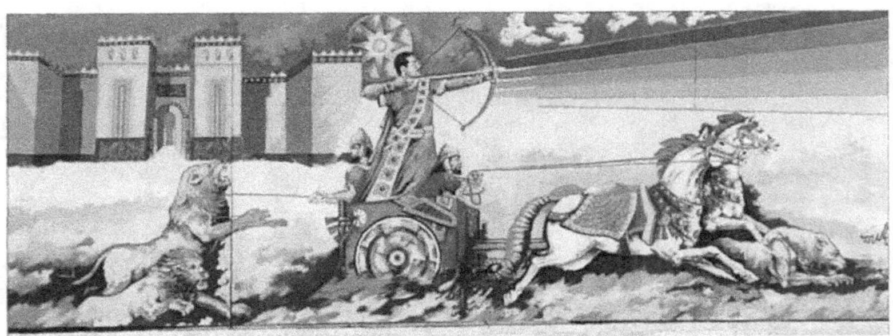

20. Saddam Hussein in the guise of an ancient Assyrian king hunting lions. The billboard, now destroyed, once stood near the site of Nineveh.

inaugurated an annual spring festival in Mosul modeled on a ritual formerly celebrated in ancient Nineveh.°

Saddam's engagement with the past was not limited to pictorial reworkings and festive revivals. Actual ancient Mesopotamian objects played a more prominent political role in Baʿathist Iraq than ever before. "The stele of Hammurabi awaits impatiently in the Louvre and the library of Ashurbanipal is in the British Museum," an article in *Al-Thawra* lamented. "Their inability to return to the homeland from which they emerged is a cultural calamity and a major crime."[38] The official Baʿath newspaper announced Iraq's determination "to restore the treasures which are the symbol of the first and greatest civilizations in human history." That the Iraqi demands for repatriation proved futile is beside the point; even unsuccessful demands roused the national spirit. The Baʿath also earmarked extensive resources for new excavation and reconstruction.

By the mid-1970s, Saddam's regime had built new archaeologi-

°These efforts to resurrect the great pagan heritage of Assyria and Babylonia did not escape the notice of Islamist critics; an article from June 1981 in the Egyptian magazine *Al-Mukhtar al-Islami* pointed to them as proof of Baʿath "sterility," "atheism," and "total bankruptcy."

cal museums throughout the country and renovated older ones, including the museum in Mosul. Saddam also spearheaded a massive construction project, a loose interpretation of ancient Babylon that blurred the line between restoration and Las Vegas–style simulacrum, with bricks bearing the inscription "This was built by Saddam, son of Nebuchadnezzar, to glorify Iraq." As pilgrimage destinations for Iraqi schoolchildren and visiting dignitaries, these museums and reconstructed archaeological sites played a central role in Baʿathist educational and diplomatic endeavors.

So completely did Saddam succeed in making the antique past his own that those who grew up under his regime sometimes find it difficult to distinguish between ancient and modern. I once asked an Iraqi grocery store owner living in Chicago about recent events in and around Mosul. He had been bused to Nineveh and Babylon as a child but now dismissed the destruction of antiquities as no great loss. "That stuff's all just Saddamist propaganda," he said.

On April 9, 2003, three weeks into the American-led invasion of Iraq and a day before the National Museum was looted, a crowd gathered around a statue of Saddam Hussein in Baghdad's Firdaws Square (figure 21). A handful of Iraqis, including the world-class wrestler and weightlifter Kadhem Sharif, took turns wielding a sledgehammer against its base. "The media is watching the Iraqis trying to topple this icon of Saddam Hussein," US Marine Corps officer Bryan McCoy later recalled, but the sledgehammer alone wasn't up to the task. "Let's give them a hand," McCoy decided, and ordered his men to use an M-88 Hercules—a tow truck for tanks equipped with a crane—to finish the job.[39]

Opinion remains divided on whether the event was spontaneous or entirely staged by the Americans. Either way, what took place at Firdaws Square was neither unique (similar removals of Saddam's image had been taking place throughout the country) nor particularly impressive (the crowd consisted of, at most, a few hundred

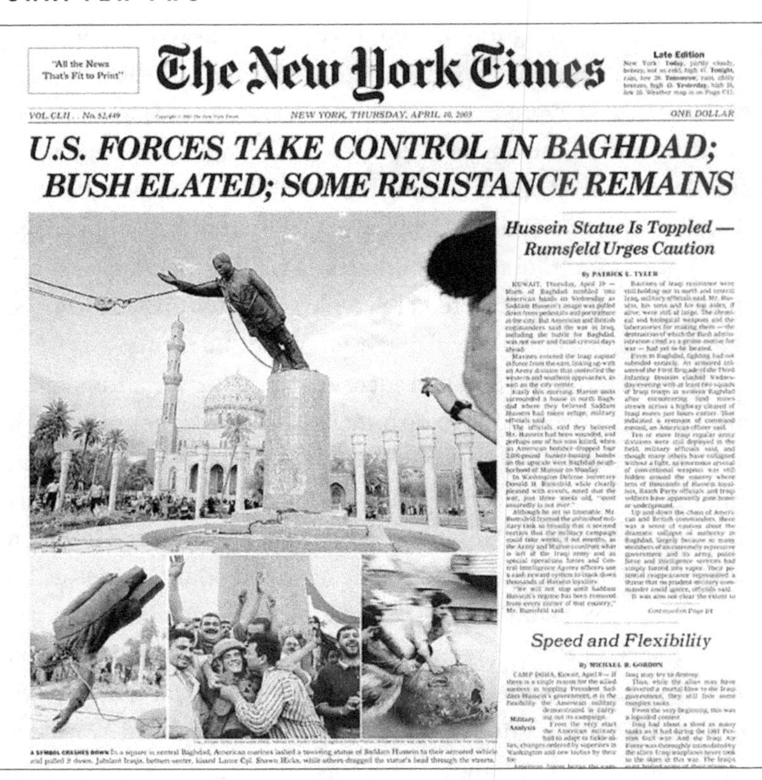

"All the News That's Fit to Print"

The New York Times

Late Edition

VOL. CLII . . No. 52,449 — NEW YORK, THURSDAY, APRIL 10, 2003 — ONE DOLLAR

U.S. FORCES TAKE CONTROL IN BAGHDAD; BUSH ELATED; SOME RESISTANCE REMAINS

Hussein Statue Is Toppled — Rumsfeld Urges Caution

By PATRICK E. TYLER

Speed and Flexibility

By MICHAEL R. GORDON

21. Front page of the *New York Times*, April 10, 2003.

people). What set Firdaws Square apart, however, was the media coverage. The toppling, which lasted about two hours, was shown live on cable news networks around the world, and its climactic moment was replayed throughout the course of the day. Newspaper and magazine covers followed with photographs of the event. In his voiceover commentary to the video footage, one reporter at Fox News said, "You have to think that there are going to be some minds changed as a result of these incredible pictures."[40] Nobody complained about the destruction of Iraqi cultural heritage.

The invasion of Iraq set off a bloodletting that has eviscerated local traditions at least as old as any Assyrian statue. In *The Corpse Washer*, Baghdad-born novelist Sinan Antoon (b. 1967) mourns the disintegration of his country. "History is a struggle of statues and monuments," Jawad, the novel's protagonist, imagines telling his deceased father. "Even Saddam's huge statue in Firdaws Square was brought down right after your death. I thought I would be happy since I detested him so much, but I felt robbed of the happiness. That was not the end I had imagined."[41] Taught in school that art originated in ancient Iraq, Jawad dreams of becoming an artist like his namesake Jawad Salim. Circumstances compel him instead to succeed his father as a ritual corpse washer in the local Shiite *mghaysil*. Unprecedented sectarian violence following the invasion yields a never-ending flow of corpses. The ambitions of Salim's Baghdad Modern Art Group now seem fantastical and give way, in this new Iraq where "even the statues are too terrified to sleep at night lest they wake up as ruins," to the modest yet noble art of the corpse washer.

And yet, a new generation of Iraqi visual artists has emerged to reimagine their country. Sundus Abdul Hadi (b. 1984) was raised outside Iraq in a home filled with books on ancient Mesopotamia and modern Arab art. These proved essential resources as she sought to define herself as an Iraqi artist in the diaspora. In her ongoing series *The New Sumerians*, Abdul Hadi uses digital imaging to explore continuities between the carved female face of the Mask of Warka (3100 BCE) and her own face. *Ancestor*, a digital collage from 2019, similarly grapples with the links between contemporary Iraq and the country's ancient past. The work reproduces the famed "Queen of the Night" terra-cotta relief of a naked female deity (now in the British Museum) above three depictions of a devoutly dressed Muslim woman in mourning (figure 22). Does the juxtaposition make the Muslim woman into an idolater? As I read the piece, the tension gives way to a rapport between these two Iraqi women.

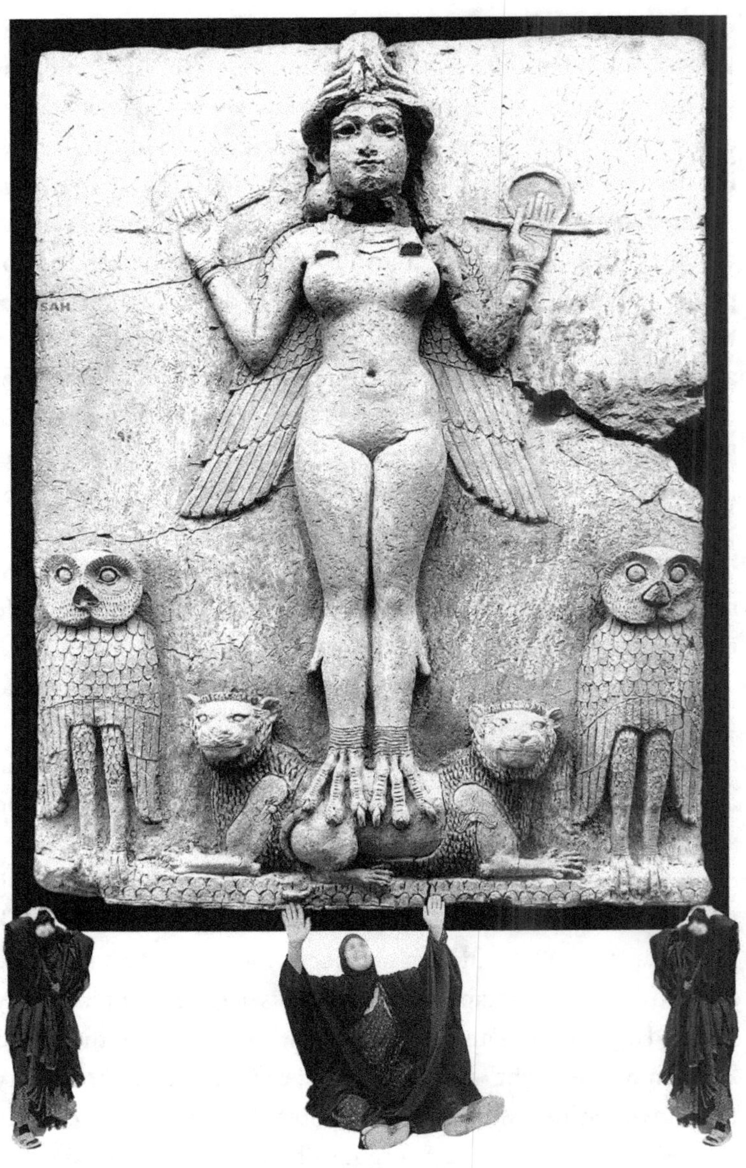

22. Sundus Abdul Hadi, *Ancestor*, 2019. Digital collage. Image courtesy of the artist.

If the future Iraq is to flourish, it won't emerge from a call to demolish the state of idols.

Like the "Queen of the Night" terra-cotta, Abdul Hadi currently resides outside Iraq. In Baghdad, other young Iraqis have been reconnecting to their country's creative traditions. In October 2019, as thousands gathered in front of Jawad Salim's Monument of Freedom to protest their government's failings and military forces responded with tear gas and live ammunition, local artists drew on an ancient heritage to make sense of the struggle. A digital reworking of Salim's monument, itself based on ancient Assyrian reliefs, showed silhouette figures dodging a tear-gas canister and broadcasting live video from a smartphone. As casualties mounted, tuk-tuk drivers and their humble three-wheeled vehicles played an essential role, shuttling the wounded away from danger. To celebrate these unexpected heroes, Wady Alrafdyn posted an image on Facebook of a tuk-tuk transformed into a *lamassu*, a protective deity from Iraq's ancient past. The image went viral.

•

From Paul-Émile Botta and Austen Henry Layard in the mid-nineteenth century to the Iraqi shopkeeper in 2010s Chicago, we all view ancient Mesopotamian objects not "objectively" but as mediated by particular impulses and conditions: imperial prestige, Enlightenment universalism, artistic modernism, nationalist self-assertion, or tyrannical oppression. Even scholars who try to be objective necessarily transform ancient objects into bearers of historical evidence whose value depends on modern commitments to the progress of knowledge. Precisely because antiquities are intimately tied to who we imagine ourselves to be, their position in the modern world remains inextricably political. Like any other political image, they make demands on their viewers. One need not endorse the destruction of antiquities to recognize how our museums enshrine them with particular meanings. Rather than turn a deaf ear when those meanings ring false, we can try to attune ourselves to their imperfections and acknowledge the ambiguities they entail.

Since 2007, Chicago-based artist Michael Rakowitz (b. 1973) has been exploring these ambiguities through his ongoing project *The Invisible Enemy Should Not Exist*. The series re-creates looted or destroyed Mesopotamian artifacts using what Rakowitz calls "the waste"—colorful packaging from Middle Eastern food products and newspapers found in Chicago's Arabic neighborhoods. [42] His use of this "detritus . . . the discarded moments of culture" alludes to the careless way antiquities have been treated but also attests to a thriving Arabic community within the United States—even if, as with his mother's family, who fled Baghdad in 1946, Arabs have not always come entirely by choice. "The more I read about the [2003 Iraq Museum] looting," Rakowitz explained in an interview, "the more complicated it became to cry about missing artifacts: for Iraqis, looting the museum and selling an artifact on the black market was a way to get out of the country."

Rakowitz's sculptures expose a host of tensions—between antiquity and modernity, homeland and diaspora, consumption and preservation, art and life. He took particular pleasure when the British Museum bought a group of his re-created artifacts, which were to be displayed alongside original artifacts from its own collection: "I'm interested in what kind of tension will be achieved between these two things." While attending a museum may be a "civilizing ritual," as the title of Carol Duncan's book puts it, Rakowitz's work helps us confront civilization's discontents without tearing down the entire edifice.

Rakowitz's sculptures were on display at the Institute for the Study of the Ancient World in New York the day ISIS released its

Mosul Museum video. Though it may be jarring to contemplate, that video constitutes a further installment in the history I have sketched here.° Through their destructive consumption of Near Eastern antiquities, ISIS has produced new images that transform the way we see those objects, imbuing them with new meanings. Nobody who has viewed the Mosul Museum video can experience ancient Mesopotamian sculpture in quite the same way again. If avant-garde art is meant to disrupt conventional ways of seeing the world, then the Islamic State's video is "good work." Indeed, the Colombian cartoonist Léon captures this aspect of ISIS by depicting one of its militants as an abstract artist exhibiting recent work in blood on canvas. In contrast to Patrick Chappatte's boorish museumgoers (figure 4), Léon's Daesh fighter does not just consume art—he creates it.

Léon's cartoon was selected from more than a thousand submissions to the 2015 International Daesh Cartoon & Caricature Contest to be displayed at Tehran's Palestine Museum of Contemporary Art. Other winning cartoons also emphasized Islamic State image-making. At least two showed a jihadist holding a weapon to the throat of a hostage. In Indian cartoonist Vivek Menon's version, a clapperboard like those used on movie sets marks the scene as a performance staged for the camera; in another, the ISIS member holds a smartphone in his free hand to take a selfie. In

°By no means the last chapter in this story, the ISIS video quickly spawned artistic responses. The Iranian-born artist Morehshin Allahyari's *Material Speculation: ISIS*, for instance, reconstructed twelve of the artifacts destroyed in the Mosul Museum using 3D printing. Each object is rendered in ghostly translucent resin and houses a memory card containing information about the ancient artifact. Michael Rakowitz's *The Invisible Enemy Should Not Exist*, which began by reproducing artifacts looted from the Iraq Museum in 2003, now also includes replicas of Mesopotamian antiquities destroyed by ISIS. In 2018, Rakowitz unveiled a reconstruction of the demolished Nineveh *lamassu* made from over ten thousand empty cans of Iraqi date syrup, in London's Trafalgar Square (figure 23).

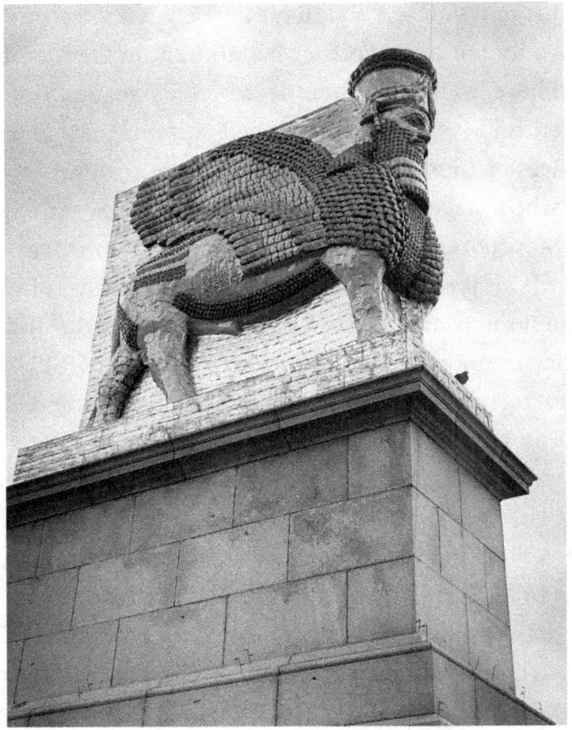

23. Michael Rakowitz, *The Invisible Enemy Should Not Exist*, 2018. Fourth Plinth Trafalgar Square. Photo: Aaron Tugendhaft.

Iranian cartoonist Hamed Bazrafkan's submission, two menacing militants stand side by side, one armed with a scimitar and the other with a bloodstained Facebook logo (figure 24). "When you find yourself surrounded by hell," Jordanian cartoonist Jehad Awartani said in an interview for *Newsweek*, "you have no other option than to fight it with all the arms at your disposal."[43] Among Awartani's many cartoons satirizing the Islamic State is an image showing a black-clad jihadist, hands covered in blood, accepting an Oscar for his artistic achievements. (As it happens, Natalie Portman once told the *Hollywood Reporter* that she hid her own Oscar when she was teaching her son about Abraham's refusal to worship idols.)

The ISIS media obsession caricatured in these cartoons is equally at play in the destruction of antiquities. The hammer wielders are attentive videographers. The video from the Mosul Museum does more than merely record the destruction of images, and its ISIS "stars" did more than simply smash sculptures. They filmed themselves doing so, edited the video, set some sequences in slow motion and sped up others, added a soundtrack and screen titles, and uploaded the finished work onto the internet. This atten-

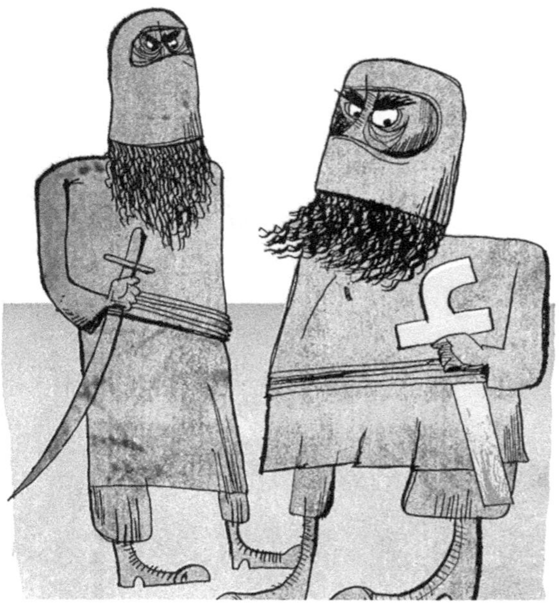

24. Hamed Bazrafkan, cartoon of Islamic State fighters, 2015.

tion to form serves to mediate our experience of ancient Mesopotamian sculpture in new ways. But that is not all. Once recognized as more than just the record of a destructive act, the video itself becomes a kind of replacement image. The destruction of images becomes part of image production.

3
Videos

ICONOCLASM DOES NOT remove images so much as generate new ones. From the French Revolution to the Chinese Cultural Revolution to the recent campaign to remove Confederate monuments in the United States, acts of iconoclasm have survived through the depiction of those acts. Since Italian futurist artist F. T. Marinetti's 1909 call to demolish museums with picks and hammers, images of image destruction have been a mainstay of the avant-garde. Much earlier, in the sixteenth and seventeenth centuries, both Protestants and Catholics produced hundreds of woodcuts, engravings, and oil paintings depicting iconoclasm that circulated throughout Europe and beyond. Why keep older images around by depicting their destruction? What work do these images of iconoclasm do for the regimes that produce them?

The Mosul Museum video produced by ISIS immediately reminded me of an image in Paul-Émile Botta's *Monument de Ninive*: a depiction of three men with sledgehammers hacking at the statue of a king. The original Assyrian relief is now lost; it may have eroded due to exposure or sunk to the bottom of the Tigris during a scuffle with locals when the French were loading crates intended for the Louvre. Thankfully, the artist Eugène Flandin copied the relief in situ at Khorsabad, the Assyrian capital in the time of Sargon II. In his drawing, three Assyrian soldiers surround a collapsed statue, its arms now lying to the side. The figure's hornless, conical helmet suggests that the statue once exalted a local king.

A caption connects the scene to the sacking of Musasir during Sargon II's 714 BCE campaign against the kingdom of Urartu (biblical Ararat) in the Armenian highlands. Though unidentified, the statue being destroyed likely depicted the Urartian king Rusa. On returning from his campaign, Sargon boasted of his accomplishments in a letter addressed to Assyria's national god Assur. He speaks of capturing Musasir, looting its palace and temple, and deporting many of its people. Sargon says nothing about destroying images. Yet years later, when designing the decorative program for his new palace, Assyrian artisans included the iconoclastic episode when depicting their king's victory. The depiction saves from oblivion what his soldiers succeeded in destroying. Why thwart that success by commemorating the act of destruction? Why decorate the palace with an image that acknowledges the existence of alternative political images?

The iconoclastic episode is part of a larger relief panel (figure 25). The immediate context shows Assyrian soldiers hauling off metal furnishings and two royal functionaries operating a large scale. Some scholars have suggested that the statue is being broken up for metal scrap—not simply destroyed but converted back into its raw material. To an Assyrian way of thinking, images of kings possessed *melammu*, an awe-inspiring radiance that emanated from kings and permeated the symbols of their royal power. By treating the Urartian king's image as nothing more than the metals

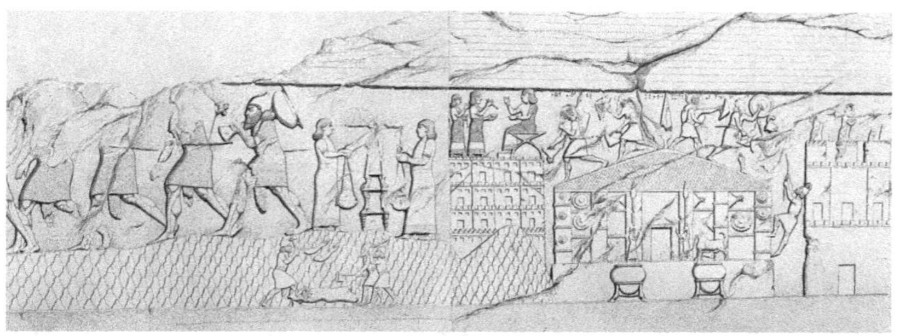

25. The sacking of Musasir. Drawing by Eugène Flandin after a relief from Sargon II's palace at Khorsabad (eighth century BCE). Composite image based on two plates from Paul-Émile Botta, *Monument de Ninive*, 1849.

from which it was fashioned, the Assyrian relief denies it this affective power. Rusa's statue joins the stockpile of plundered silver and gold Sargon will use to build his royal palace—a process depicted on its walls.

Sargon's son Sennacherib complemented his father's image of image destruction with images of image creation. His reliefs depict workmen in various national costumes quarrying stone, carving the *lamassu* figures for his palace gates, and transporting the colossal sculptures (figure 8).° The "king of the world" thus boasts that conquered subjects from all over the world have come together to construct the image of Assyrian rule. But any individuality or diver-

°In chapter 2, I mentioned the frontispiece to Austen Henry Layard's *Nineveh and Its Remains*, which depicts the removal and transport of Sennacherib's bull colossi to London—celebrating British technical prowess in much the same way the reliefs had promoted Assyrian achievements. In a subsequent book, *Discoveries in the Ruins of Nineveh and Babylon* (1853), the Englishman describes the ancient scene, informed no doubt by his own experience: "Although these rollers materially facilitated the motion, it would be almost impossible, when passing over rough ground, or if the rollers were jammed, to give the first impetus to so heavy a body by mere force applied to the cables." Layard was clearly impressed by the engineering feats of his predecessors.

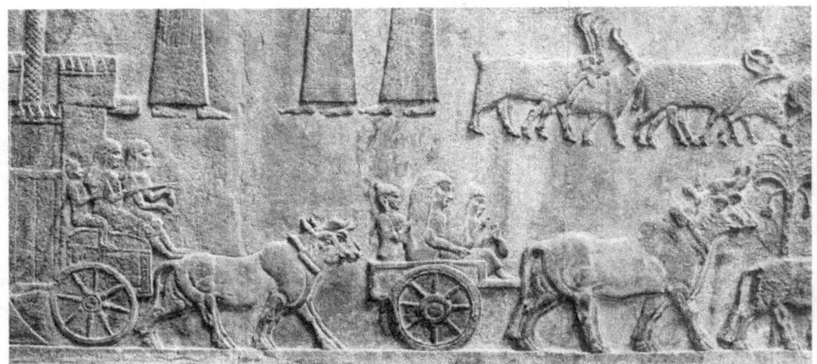

26. Family of deportees leaving a captured Babylonian city on an ox-cart. Detail from wall decoration of Tiglath-pileser III's Central Palace in Kalhu (Nimrud), later reused in Esarhaddon's Southwest Palace. British Museum, ANE 118882.

sity their costumes may once have represented has been stripped away by the Assyrian whip; the men are reduced to raw labor, just as Rusa's statue is reduced to raw materials.

The relief illustrates not just technological achievement but a massive administrative program that affected over 1.5 million people. Assyrian policy aimed to erode local patriotic allegiance while promoting economic efficiency. Administrators directed laborers where they were most needed, much as the free labor market is said to do today. Whether these "human resources" were depicted as willing migrants on their way to new jobs (figure 26) or lines of workers straining to haul bull colossi to the palace, Assyrian resettlement policy transformed culturally distinct members of local communities into deracinated human capital serving the needs of a unified global economy. In an empire that historian Karen Radner has recently compared to a modern multinational corporation, political discord gave way to economic unity—or so the viewers of imperial imagery were meant to believe.

Sargon II's palace idealized the imperial ambition to unify the entire world. "On great limestone slabs," its inscriptions declare, "I engraved the countries conquered by my own hand, and I placed them along the base of the walls, making them objects of admiration. By the skill of the sculptors, I adorned the inside of those palaces with the people of the countries conquered by the power of Assur my lord, from west to east."[1] By unseating false kings and eradicating unjust ways of life, Sargon would enable all mankind to "be of one mouth"—a boast that echoes the biblical account of Babel. The end of political opposition would, like the elimination of images, usher in a world without politics.

Assyrian imagery reached far beyond the palace walls. Just as photography today makes works of art accessible to those who cannot travel to see them in a museum, cylinder seals disseminated the iconography of the Assyrian palace to those who never visited it. Seals depicting a ritual scene with a sacred tree, for example, replicated reliefs in Ashurnasirpal II's throne room at Nimrud. Others showing the royal hunt echoed the same palace relief that would inspire Saddam Hussein's self-presentation in the guise of an Assyrian king (figure 20). Such seals proliferated the image of Assyrian kingship by creating an "imaginary palace" that spread royal imagery wherever they, and documents bearing their impressions, circulated.

Assyrian kings also imprinted themselves on the natural landscape. Sennacherib had his image carved into the remote cliffs overlooking the Gomel River at Khennis (figure 27). Similar rock reliefs dot the extremities of the Assyrian empire in all directions. Perhaps best known are the Nahr al Kalb reliefs in present-day Lebanon. When Esarhaddon passed there in 671 BCE on his way to conquering Egypt, the cliff already sported three thirteenth-century BCE relief steles of the pharaoh Ramses II. The Assyrian ruler added his own stele-shaped relief next to his Egyptian predecessor's

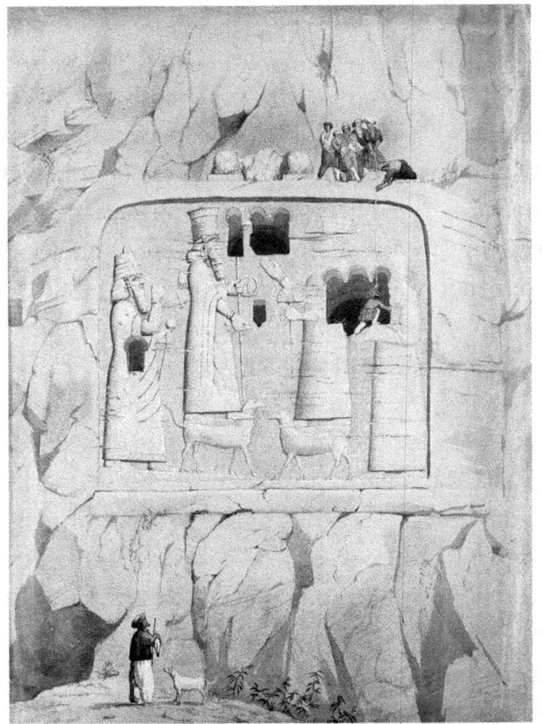

27. Watercolor illustration showing A. H. Layard climbing over the main rock relief at Khennis (704–681 BCE), Iraqi Kurdistan, 1853.

(figure 28), thereby affirming the Assyrian capacity to transform nature's chaos into a realm of order, justice, and prosperity—even where it was evident that other kings had sought to do so as well. (The practice of rulers adding relief carvings at Nahr al Kalb has continued—from ancient Babylonian, Hellenistic, and Roman emperors to Napoleon III and Hezbollah.)

However forcefully regimes may try to eradicate rivals, none has yet attained a universal monopoly on images. No "king of totality" has produced images so total that they preclude alternatives. Nimrud's world-state, with one set of images for all, is not so easy to achieve. The images of conquered regimes stubbornly persevere, and new images inevitably arise. Regimes must therefore choose between ignoring and acknowledging images that (implicitly or not) call their own into question. Unable to eradicate competing images, the best a regime may be able to do is to delegitimize them.

Sargon's iconoclastic palace relief at once admits an alternative way of imagining the world and shows the weakness of that alternative. Assyrian soldiers strike down one physical sculpture, and the image of that destruction strikes at the power of many more. It serves as a warning against the temptation of false images and as a reminder that only the Assyrian king—reveling in his universal dominion—can realize truth and justice. Assyrian iconography creates a political community around a king whose monopoly on

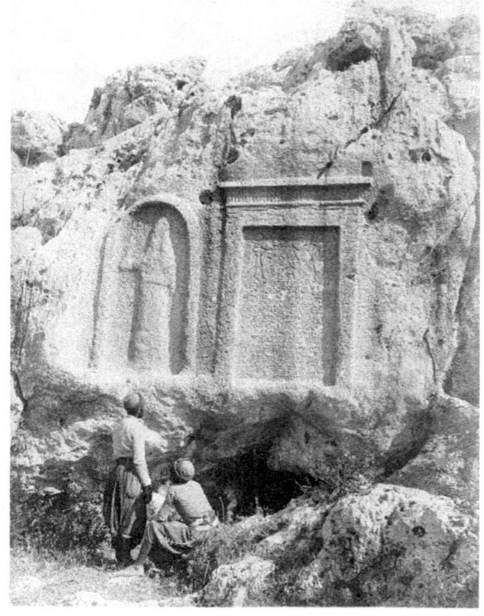

28. Rock reliefs at Nahr al Kalb, Lebanon. Photograph from an early twentieth-century postcard.

truth and justice denies the need for politics. Opposition appears only as insurgence.

●

As we've seen, the relief carving of image smashing is but one detail of an extensive Assyrian iconographic program. The ISIS video of image smashing is likewise but one episode in a broader program of image production, which also includes videos of decapitations, military victories, acts of pious devotion, and the technocratic functioning of everyday life in the Islamic State. As in the Assyrian relief, the destruction of old images manifesting one political vision becomes a component in a new set of political images manifesting another. Old images are not erased. They are recycled.

A few weeks after the Mosul Museum video appeared, ISIS released a video of barrel bombs detonating next to relief panels of winged genies in Ashurnasirpal II's palace at nearby Nimrud (figures 29 and 30). Again, the destruction of ancient images, which had established the parameters of Assyrian political imagination, contributes to the production of a new set of images meant to define a new polity. These new images furbish a new kind of wall on the screens of our laptops and smartphones (figure 31). ISIS has built its own palace appropriate to our digital age, an onscreen palace simultaneously everywhere and nowhere. From this palace, the Islamic State has sought to define the House of Islam.

The group's Al Hayat Media Center has been chiefly responsible for the construction of this new palace. Using a teardrop-shaped logo that resembles that of Al Jazeera, Al Hayat produces slick, sophisticated videos in several languages and multiple formats—from minute-long, Twitter-friendly "Mujatweets" to hour-long documentary-style films. It also published *Dabiq*, the online magazine that claimed (as noted in chapter 1) that Ibrahim "was not concerned about the feelings and sentiments of his people

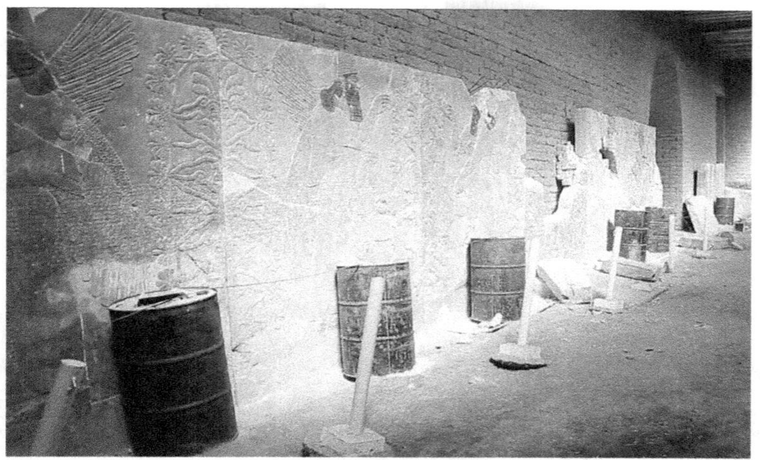

29. Islamic State preparations to blow up Assyrian palace reliefs at Nimrud. Video released April 12, 2015.

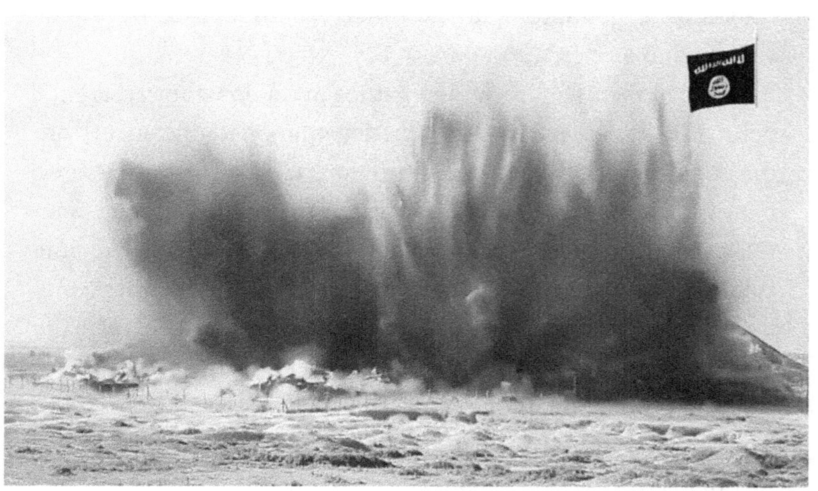

30. Islamic State explosion of the Assyrian palace at Nimrud. Video released April 12, 2015.

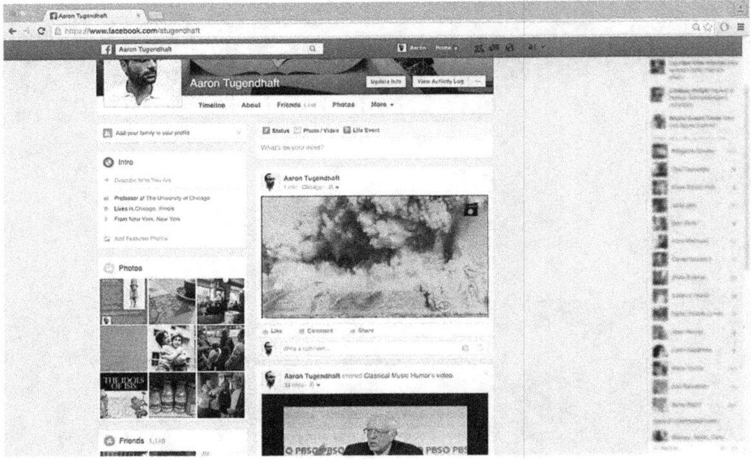

31. The destruction of Nimrud as seen on Facebook.

when he destroyed their idols." This diverse programming playfully repackages and repurposes imagery from visual traditions ancient and modern.

First-person shooter video games are a constant reference point. ISIS has appropriated marketing images, for instance, from the popular franchise *Call of Duty* (figure 32). And user-generated modifications of the game allow players to don the persona of an ISIS militant engaged in combat against Westerners, Syrian regime soldiers, and Kurdish peshmerga fighters. The ISIS video depicting the destruction of Nimrud's ruins itself echoes an episode, set in the 1980s, from *Call of Duty: Black Ops 2*, in which the game's protagonist, US Special Forces operative Alex Mason, travels to Afghanistan to gather information about archvillain Raul Menendez. Fighting alongside the mujahideen, Mason must blow up part of a structure in order to block a Soviet advance (figure 33). The building resembles the twelfth-century madrassa complex Gumbad-i Chisht-e Sharif. (The campaign opens with Mason looking up as his partner rappels down the Bamiyan Buddhas—famed, by the time of the game's release in 2012, for their destruction by the Taliban more than a decade earlier.)

When I began this project, I used research funds to buy a PlayStation gaming console and a copy of *Call of Duty*. Lacking the skill to progress beyond the first campaign, I asked one of my students

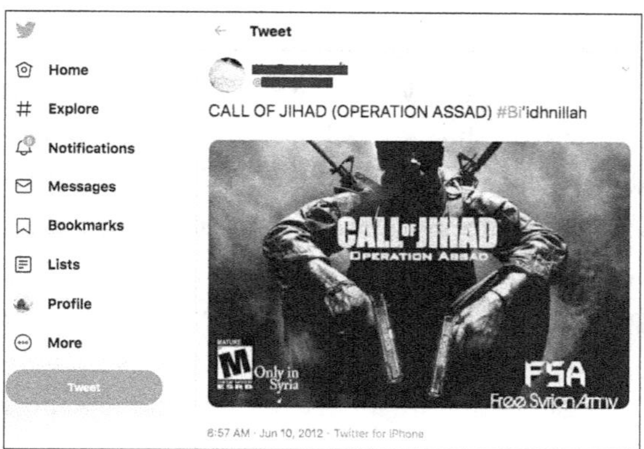

32. "Call of Jihad: Operation Assad." Meme circulating on Twitter based on promotional material for the video game *Call of Duty*.

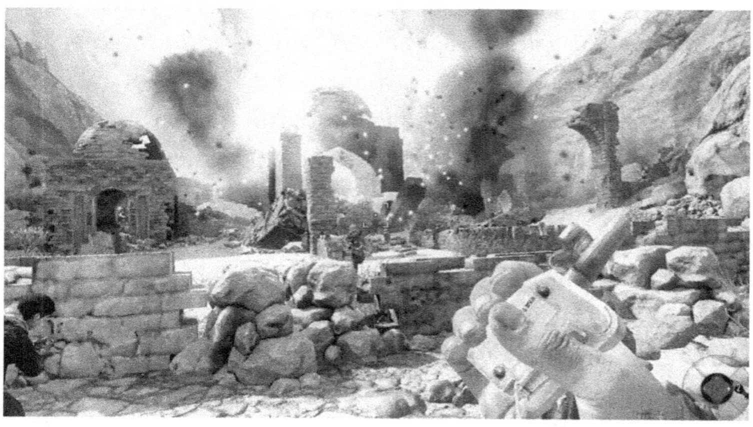

33. A gamer playing Alex Mason explodes a medieval Islamic architectural complex in *Call of Duty: Black Ops 2*.

to identify moments in popular first-person shooter games that corresponded to scenes in Islamic State videos. In addition to the *Black Ops 2* scene just mentioned, he identified parallel depictions of aerial bombardment, drive-by shootings (à la *Grand Theft Auto*), and an elaborate interrogation scene.

Many of these images originate not in the imagination of American video game programmers but in media coverage of American wars. Anyone who came of age watching news coverage of the 1990–1991 Persian Gulf War, as I did, can't fail to associate aerial bombardment with the new vision of warfare offered by camera-equipped "smart bombs." Similarly, the prisoner's orange jumpsuit in the interrogation scene pulls directly from images of prisoners at Guantanamo Bay following the invasions of Iraq and Afghanistan.

In reproducing such images in its videos, ISIS intentionally mirrors images of American imperialism. In other words, ISIS videos imitate video games that are themselves imitations of the real world. This does not mean that one somehow returns through them to the real world itself. The play element of the video game is preserved in the world ISIS imagines—albeit with serious consequences.

In June 2012, ISIS began to release a series of videos on the internet called *Saleel al-Sawarim* (*Clanging of the Swords*). The first installments were rather wooden compilations of polemical speeches and combat footage. But the fourth, released in May 2014, displays greater rhetorical sophistication. Stylistically mimicking sequences from combat video games, the hour-long video opens with a computer-generated satellite image of the Middle East that zooms into drone-shot aerial footage of Fallujah. A dizzying spin immerses the viewer in street-to-street fighting at the very heart of the Islamic State's world. By imitating the first-person shooter perspective, subsequent scenes reiterate the video-game quality of life in the Caliphate. The final sequence shows a man walking across a peaceful field, carrying a large ISIS flag fluttering gloriously in the wind. As in a video game's metastory, *Saleel al-Sawarim 4* closes with an image of justice triumphant.

One ISIS fighter told a BBC journalist that his new life in the Caliphate was "better than that game *Call of Duty*."[2] Videos like *Saleel al-Sawarim 4* provide a glimpse of the kind of world ISIS offers its adherents—a world already familiar to those who have grown up on video games and have sometimes been recruited through online gaming networks. The Islamic State's recourse to a video-game idiom has consequently been interpreted as a recruitment technique.

Though true as far as it goes, this interpretation seems too simple. Why would someone wish permanently to inhabit a first-person shooter video game?

In *Homo Ludens* (1938), a classic treatise on play, the Dutch historian Johan Huizinga defines play as "a voluntary activity or occupation executed within certain fixed limits of time and place, according to rules freely accepted but absolutely binding, having its aim in itself and accompanied by a feeling of tension, joy, and consciousness that it is different from ordinary life."[3] First-person shooter video games exhibit these characteristics. The gaming console, which can be turned on or off at will, both provides a place for play and circumscribes play within a finite time. One is free not to play, but once playing one must accept the game's rules.

Play, Huizinga writes, brings a "temporary, limited perfection" into an imperfect world. It creates an order in which political action is neither needed nor possible. That temporary escape from politics becomes permanent in the world Islamic State videos imagine. Instead of "standing quite consciously outside 'ordinary' life," the Islamic State's play-space is coextensive with ordinary life—to the degree such a life can still be called ordinary. Yet we lose an essential part of ourselves when we cannot stop playing. Huizinga recognized the horrors that accompany unending play. Writing on the eve of World War II, he saw no redemption in "the spectacle of a society rapidly goose-stepping into helotry."[4] ISIS videos, like fascist pageants, draw us into a world with no exit from play. They promise viewers a transformation like the one undergone by the protagonist of the dystopian online series *My Life as a Video Game*, an incessant gamer who finds himself pulled into the world of the games he plays.[°]

Video games give players explicit, unambiguous tasks. In *Black Ops 2*, for instance, Alex Mason is tasked with gathering intel on the Menendez cartel. Toward this end, he must investigate Raul Menendez's connection with the Soviets, defend a mujahideen base, retake a weapons cache, and interrogate a Russian prisoner. All of these actions are embedded within the game's metastory: the need to bring Menendez to justice for his anti-American activities. Players choose the steps to take to accomplish each task. Head right or left? Use the AK-47 assault rifle or a Makarov pistol? But one never considers whether the tasks are worth pursuing in the first place. Doing so would be senseless. Since the goals are encoded into the game-world, one can either accept them or not play. The game allows a player to focus on local success without examining final ends. It lacks, in other words, the prerequisite for political life: evaluating what constitutes the good for a group of people living together. Players cannot design alternative ends for communal life

° Strictly speaking, one is no longer "playing" once inside the game. Adapting terminology from film theory, media theorist Alexander Galloway distinguishes between "diegetic" and "nondiegetic" video-game actions. Diegetic actions involve characters and events that are presumed to exist within the game's narrative world; nondiegetic actions are external to the pretend world of character and story but still part of the game. For example, nobody within the game-world presses Pause, but pressing Pause is as much part of a first-person shooter game as firing a weapon. Nondiegetic actions occur at the border between the narrative world of the game and the world we inhabit in everyday life. That is where actual gameplay occurs. Within the diegetic realm, one isn't so much playing as being played (either by the machine or its operator). ISIS videos only appear to offer a world of play. In the Caliphate, one can never press Pause.

or initiate action to bring about change. They cannot be—indeed, do not wish to be—political. Obedience to the unambiguous rules of a video game offers an attractive alternative to the difficult choices and ambiguities of political life. Life within a video game resembles Ibrahim's regime without images—a life of unmediated obedience to the programmer's all-encompassing law.

Life on the ground in ISIS-controlled northern Iraq in 2015 didn't actually resemble a video game. Like Assyria's imperial artisans, Al Hayat Media Center produces images meant to mold political identity rather than to depict reality. Both the ancient Assyrian palace and its contemporary avatar offer viewers political images that obscure the human capacity for political judgment and responsibility. They generate political communities, but at the expense of producing citizens who do not conceive of themselves as political beings.

But alternative images that would encourage us to think politically remain possible. "Every image of man is defined against other possibilities," writes political theorist Wendy Brown in *Undoing the Demos*. "Even when one image becomes hegemonic, it carves itself against a range of other possibilities—tacitly arguing with them, keeping them at bay, or subordinating them."[5]

•

By imagining the Caliphate as a first-person shooter video game, ISIS videos tempt viewers with the possibility of an escape from politics. So do the social networks that deliver those videos to our screens.

Consider al-Farabi's tenth-century idealized portrait of a prophet who decides on appropriate political images and disseminates them to the people. With his intimate knowledge of people's desires and likes, the prophet engineers images that structure social interactions and channel civic activity toward the regime's defined good.

This making of prophetic images is a top-down, one-way affair. The people take no part in producing the images that govern their lives. In its ideal form, the Assyrian empire operated similarly. The king and his advisers designed the palace's visual programs, which provided the people with shared images of the good.

But when we come to palaces built on the internet, matters become more complicated. Web 2.0 revolutionized how users interact with online content. With older websites (retroactively designated Web 1.0), proprietors posted content and users simply viewed or downloaded it. Content creators were few; most of us were passive consumers. As the millennium turned, new types of websites started to appear. Interactive platforms such as Facebook, YouTube, Instagram, Twitter, and Snapchat have given individuals the power to exchange text, audio, and video of all kinds, not to mention tagging, linking, commenting, and sharing. The old top-down, unidirectional content flow has given way to websites made by users. With Web 2.0, every user becomes a content creator.

In 2006 *Time* magazine celebrated this new class of "produsers" by selecting "You" as its Person of the Year (figure 34). "It's a story," the magazine euphorically reported, "about the many wresting power from the few."[6] Were *Time*'s editors right about the political implications of this technological revolution? If we are no longer passive recipients of other peoples' images, have we become our own prophets, collectively engaged in determining the images that define our political lives?

Over three-quarters of adult Americans now own a smartphone, and global smartphone ownership exceeded three billion in 2020. These new tools do not merely facilitate the production and circulation of images—they shape our experience of them. Just as the Assyrian palace's physical architecture structured the experience of the images on its walls, digital platforms introduce an algorithmic architecture that determines how and when images appear

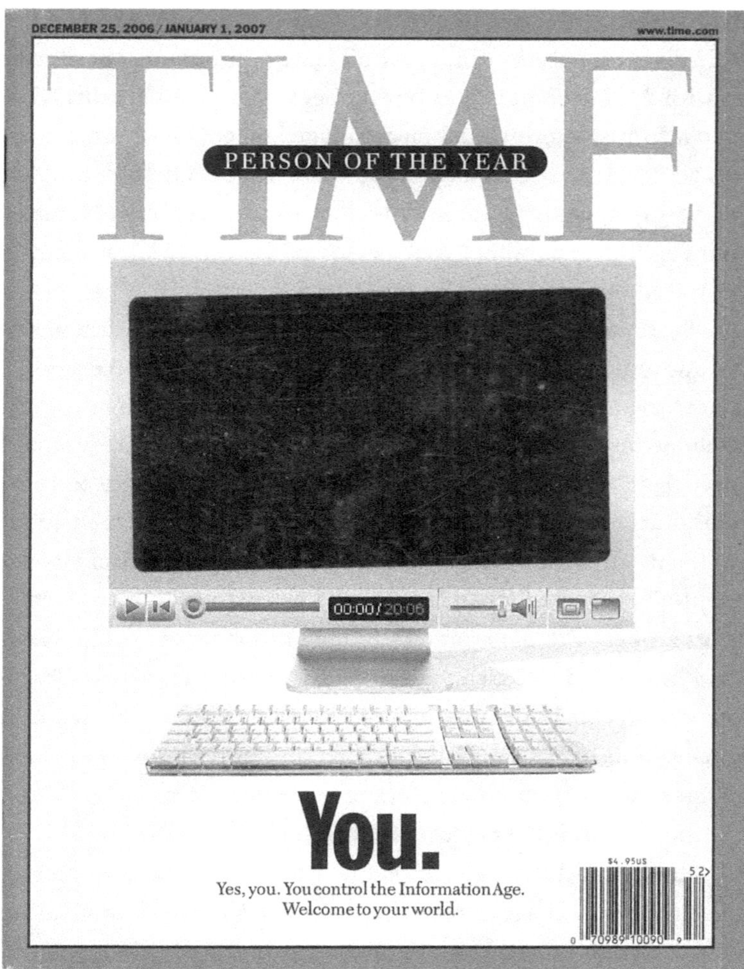

34. "Person of the Year: You." Cover of Time magazine, December 25, 2006.

onscreen. The architecture, visible or not, is at least as important as the image. An Assyrian king was ultimately responsible for both: he controlled what images were made and how they were displayed. Today, these two functions have been divided between masses of cellphone-wielding image-makers and a few corporations that own the platforms, the architecture within which our images appear. This division between those who create content and those who control display complicates how images operate politically. Digital platforms determine when an image is seen, by whom, and in what context; understanding the power of these centrally controlled platforms necessarily dampens democratic idealism. Notably, four years after naming "You" Person of the Year, *Time* magazine bestowed that distinction on Mark Zuckerberg.

The founder of Facebook bets that "a fundamental mathematical law underlying human social relationships" can solve a problem at the heart of politics—how to manage conflicting desires.[7] Whereas al-Farabi envisioned a human prophet whose images could mold people's desires and thereby generate concord between citizens, Zuckerberg advocates a machine that knows so much about us that it can direct us toward happiness. Thanks to the online data we provide, Zuckerberg's machine knows many of our characteristics far better than al-Farabi's human prophet ever could. Facebook encodes our likes and desires, and directs us toward what—according to its understanding of the mathematical law of social interactions—we want. All-knowing and automatic algorithms replace the messy political work of managing desires. Facebook, in other words, is the perfect prophet.

The data-driven algorithms that power Facebook are merely the latest wave in a long history of trying to sidestep human judgment through quantification, measurement, and rule-governed bureaucratic processes. Archaeologists have recovered cuneiform mathematical documents that attest to ancient imperial administrators using algorithms to make quantitative predictions and determine resource allocation. Assyrian bureaucrats employed mathematical abstractions, approximations, and standardizations to manage people and goods. We see these functionaries at work in Sargon's Khorsabad relief (figure 25). Alongside the soldiers breaking a statue down for its metal content are a seated official and two scribes recording the booty. The rival king's statue is reduced to raw material and then converted into data. The Assyrian king aspired to establish justice on earth through quantification and rationalization; digital technology promises to do so far more effectively.

"The decisive reason for the advance of bureaucratic organization has always been its purely technical superiority," writes sociologist Max Weber in his classic account of bureaucracy. "The fully developed bureaucratic mechanism compares with other organizations exactly as does the machine with the non-mechanical modes of production."[8] In its utopian formulation, automation circumvents the biases inherent in human decision-making. Disregarding love, hatred, and other personal, irrational, and emotional considerations, bureaucrats make decisions based on replicable calculation, *sine ira ac studio* (without scorn or bias). And they improve through constant practice. Bureaucracy thereby provides precision, speed, and the reduction of ambiguity and friction—all characteristics politics lacks. Digital technology, unknown to Weber, seems to take decision-making even further out of human hands. But algorithms don't function automatically, any more than the Golden Calf emerged fully formed from the fire. As Jaron Lanier reminds us, "Digital technology is really just people in disguise."[9]

Al-Farabi's prophet cultivates individuals so that they can share a life in common. Algorithmic prophets, by contrast, adapt the world to each individual. "A squirrel dying in front of your house may be more relevant to your interests than people dying in Africa," Zuckerberg notoriously remarked.[10] You want squirrels, you get squirrels. On unveiling Facebook's redesigned news feed in 2013, Zuckerberg said the platform strives to provide everyone in the world with the best personal newspaper. Calibrated to individual interests and desires, every news feed is unique. Algorithms filter the data users produce and shape it into customized streams of information. Facebook's news feed mimics the Middle East peace plan announced in the satirical newspaper the *Onion*: "Everyone in Middle East Given Own Country in 317,000,000-State Solution."[11] Facebook goes to the opposite extreme of Nimrud's homogenous world-state; both overcome the problem of politics but at the expense of human freedom.

Social media hasn't yet succeeded in sealing us off completely. Internet trolls periodically unsettle the comfort of our algorithmically produced cells, just as barbarians always frustrated Assyrian aspirations to unite the world. Besides, not everyone's interests are limited to the squirrel in their front yard. Many of us want to engage the wider world in speech and action, and we often do so through social media. People regularly post and share content that identifies and defines issues of public concern. Facebook and Twitter have been used to organize activists around the globe. And online images constantly compete to exert their political power over us. People still act politically, and they do so online.

It is tempting, then, to imagine our shared online space not as a palace but as an agora, the meeting ground in an ancient Greek polis where adult male citizens could exchange opinions as equals. (It was also where Socrates made himself a nuisance, prodding fellow citizens to question what they liked to think they already knew.) The agora gave political freedom a spatial structure. Online platforms seem to open the agora to everyone (who can afford and access an internet connection) and thereby radically expand the space for practicing politics—even if users are in a constant race against algorithms programmed to constrict their reach.

"The hallmark of [ancient] non-political communities," Hannah Arendt writes in *The Human Condition*, "was that their public place, the agora, was not a meeting place of citizens, but a market place where craftsmen could show and exchange products."[12] To discourage citizens from engaging in public affairs, Greek tyrants tried to transform the agora into merely an assemblage of shops. Economically engaged, the people under a tyrant's rule would, he hoped, refrain from asserting themselves politically. The diversity of perspectives that gain voice in political space would give way to the unity of the tyrant's personal interest. Though a city could flourish materially under a tyrant, his arrival meant an end to freedom.

Tech giants accomplish something similar with their algorithms, but with a twist. Political action isn't replaced by economic activity but transformed into it. Platform providers rely on constant user activity to accumulate the data on which their profits depend. It's activity (not political action) that matters. Activity becomes data and data becomes wealth. From the data-miner's perspective, the only difference between images of your neighbor's kitten, a Bernie Sanders rally, and an ISIS beheading is how much online activity each generates. (A first-person shooter video game dictates the end for your action; a data-miner doesn't care.) The more we engage with the political images that appear on our screens, the more power we produce for those who control the platforms. The Mosul Museum video produced a spike in activity among both the euphoric and the horrified; it made the data-miners money.

Assyrian palace reliefs openly depicted the corvée labor that kings demanded from their deracinated subjects—labor in the service of the regime. Social media, by contrast, disguises our servitude. What we experience as free engagement in daily life (wishing a friend happy birthday, calling out racism in a recent film, promoting a new band), Facebook and its peers register as data. Online interfaces allow tech companies to amass power while evading the traditional pitfalls of ancient tyranny: if we feel free, we are less likely to revolt.

How will these companies handle mounting confrontations with national governments and sinking public confidence? In April 2018, Zuckerberg appeared before the United States Congress to answer questions regarding the Cambridge Analytica data-sharing scandal. That year, Facebook lost fifteen million users in the United States. (Some left for hipper platforms; others sought an escape from social media altogether.) Zuckerberg has since acknowledged that without an improved regulatory framework "people are just going to get angrier and angrier [and will] eventually just say, 'Screw it, take a hammer to the whole thing.'"[13] Perhaps. But so long as we stay plugged in, Zuckerberg and his friends have us working for them—even when we are protesting against them.

Though political acts abound online, they lose efficacy when coopted into a system of mathematical control. Images reduced to data are drained of their *melammu*. A new form of iconoclasm breaks images down for their content without need of a hammer. This invisible iconoclasm raises no outcry. And yet, an iconoclasm that leaves images intact poses no less a threat to our freedom.

Coda

IN THE WEEKS LEADING up to his mental collapse in 1889, Friedrich Nietzsche composed *Twilight of the Idols; or, How to Philosophize with a Hammer*. "Posing questions with a *hammer* and, perhaps, hearing in reply that famous hollow sound," Nietzsche writes, "what a pleasure for me, an old psychologist and pied piper; in my presence, the very things that want to keep quiet are *made to speak out*."[1] Nietzsche neither venerates idols nor smashes them; instead, he taps them "as with a tuning fork."

The idols that concern Nietzsche are those of Western philosophy: "the oldest, most convinced, puffed-up, and fat-headed idols you will ever find." But the figure of the idol-tapper suggests an attitude that can be extended to all of the images that orient us. As Ibrahim knew, all images are incomplete. But he was too impatient to tap Nimrud's idols. Hammer in hand, he never gave them a chance to speak. Had Ibrahim grasped that images are coy, not dumb, he might have used his hammer to sound them out instead of destroying them. Had he tapped them lightly as with a tuning fork, they might have divulged something to Ibrahim and his neighbors about the regime they were living under and its possible alternatives.

We will neither live in a regime without images nor find images that aren't the work of human hands. The best we can do is embrace the ongoing task of deciding which imperfect images to live with. Unlike Ibrahim's neighbors, we don't have to serve unthinkingly the images we've inherited; we can take a step back to ask whether those images suit our needs. We can become our own prophets not by incessantly posting photos to the Web but by taking collective responsibility for the images with which we surround ourselves.

In order to evaluate our images, we must discover what they conceal. We must sound out what they (and we) would prefer to keep silent. How do we determine where to tap? How do we break through the "second nature" that images induce and open up a space for thinking? One way is to tap images against one another—a technique I've used throughout this book.

Both the Islamic State's Mosul Museum video, from 2015, and the *Illustrated London News* engraving of the British Museum's Nineveh Room, from 1853 (figure 9), depict ways of comporting oneself in a museum. As models of behavior embedded within broader social forms, each conceals as well as reveals. The English engraving evokes respectability and sophistication. Seen on its own, it might not call up the imperialism that often attends museum-going as a cosmopolitan ideal. Tap it against the ISIS video, however, and hidden aspects of the engraving start to come into view. That doesn't make the two images equally beneficial for communal life. Judgment may rightly incline us to choose one over the other. But judgment (as opposed to knee-jerk chauvinism) requires that we discern and assess the unsavory elements of our chosen images and recognize how other images promote goods that ours cannot.

Tapping images can make us keener critics of ourselves as well as of others.

If all images are incomplete, not all are incomplete in the same way. Some, like the Mosul Museum video and the *Illustrated London News* engraving, hide their incompleteness by presenting matters as settled. Other images are overtly incomplete and pose questions more than they provide answers.

German photographer Thomas Struth (b. 1954) has been making images of visitors at some of the world's finest museums since 1989. By focusing on museumgoers, he challenges viewers of his photographs to reflect on the activity of looking at art. Struth's images draw our attention to the reverence, contemplation, and sometimes boredom people experience when visiting museums. "The photos should lead viewers away from regarding the works as mere fetish-objects and initiate their own understanding," Struth said in an interview. "Therein lies the moment of pause or questioning. Because the viewers are reflected in their activity, they have to wonder what they themselves are doing at the moment."[2]

Pergamon Museum IV, Berlin (figure 35), for instance, depicts small groups and lone museumgoers in a brightly lit room filled with fragments of ancient Greek sculpture. While the composition recalls the engraving in the *Illustrated London News*, it doesn't advertise the importance of museumgoing so much as ask us to consider why we take museumgoing so seriously. Encountered on a museum wall, Struth's large print (which measures five by seven and a half feet) confronts us with an image of people doing what we ourselves are doing—but the activity appears strange. We see *that* there are museumgoers in the picture, but we're not quite sure *why* they are there. (In the Pergamon Museum photographs, Struth intensifies this estrangement by deliberately posing the museumgoers.) Struth's photograph unsettles what we have taken

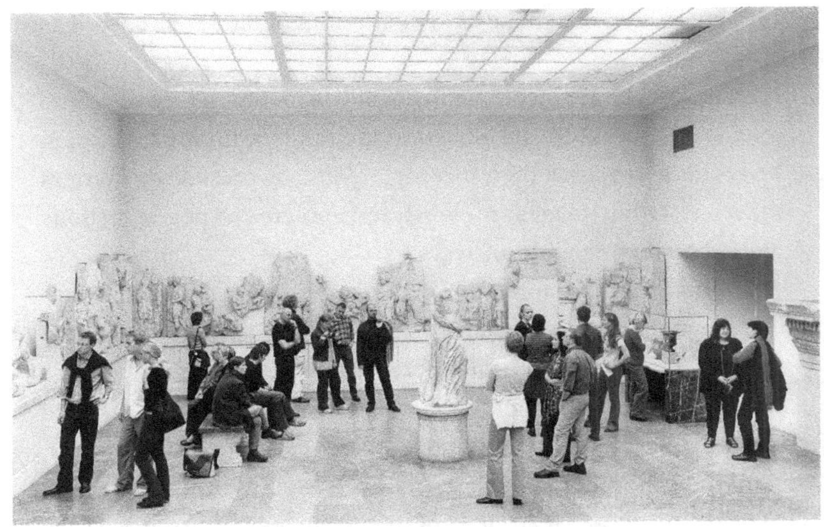

35. Thomas Struth, *Pergamon Museum IV, Berlin*, 2001. Chromogenic print, 153.4 × 228.8 cm (framed). Ed. 1/10. National Gallery of Victoria, Melbourne; purchased with the assistance of the Bowness Family Fund for Contemporary Photography, 2008 (2008.518). Image courtesy of the National Gallery of Victoria, Melbourne. © Thomas Struth.

for granted by introducing ambiguity. His image makes us wonder about ourselves.

"This wondering of yours is very much the mark of a philosopher," Socrates reportedly told the mathematician Theaetetus. "Philosophy starts nowhere else but with wondering."[3] Like Socrates, who provoked people in the agora, images can make us wonder about matters we ordinarily take for granted. Might one build a regime entirely of such wonder-inducing images? The idea may sound appealing, but the never-ending uncertainty such a regime would elicit would make life unbearable. Images that take a stand are necessary. Besides, unsettling images tend over time to become domesticated. It's easy to say that one should always be critical. The practice of self-criticism is more difficult.

As Socrates knew, a stimulus that awakens wonder can also trigger rage. Many in the agora were perfectly content with their unexamined opinions and the civic gods that grounded them. They weren't interested in tapping their city's images. Socrates's incessant questions were an unwelcome irritation. "Indeed, some say that Socrates was a troll," writes Rachel Barney in her mock-Aristotelean treatise *On Trolling*.[4] No wonder his fellow citizens put him to death.

When I first saw the Mosul Museum video, I reacted with rage, just as ISIS wanted. Their tyrannical theatrics were intended not to make me reevaluate my opinions but to entrench me in my prejudices. I was being provoked to smash back—the more outraged, the less free to exercise judgment. On rewatching the video, I recalled the Assyrian relief from Khorsabad. The uncanny resemblance called out for comparison. Curiosity pulled me out from my apolitical stupor and inarticulate rage. Suddenly, the hollowness of my own political images began to tap against the ISIS video, and to reverberate. I began to wonder, and that wonder led to this book.

Political life vitally depends on shared images that allow us to envision how we want to live together. We will live with images for as long as we remain political beings. To be free citizens, we need to think about how our political images arose, why they were chosen, and what they leave out. In that way, we become aware of our images' incompleteness without denying our need for them or pretending we didn't make them. We don't have to smash them or submit to them. We can tap them instead.

ACKNOWLEDGMENTS

Thank you to Sami Aldebri, Amichai Amit, Ewa Atanassow, Zainab Bahrani, Benjamin Balint, Orit Bashkin, Mohamed Wajdi Ben Hammed, Anastasia Berg, Rowina Bou-Harb, Shira Brisman, Claudia Brittenham, Keith Budner, Noah Chafets, Ali Cherri, Kenneth Coleman, Joshua Craze, Thomas Cummins, Lorraine Daston, Daniel Doneson, Theodor Dunkelgrun, Josh Ellenbogen, Darby English, Christopher Faraone, Eckart Frahm, Jason Frank, Ximena Fuentes, Alessandra Gilibert, Karim-Yassin Goessinger, Anthony Grafton, Annie Greene, Fiona Greenland, Emily Hammer, Ömür Harmanşah, Alana Hein, Paul Hine, Matthew Irvin, Chloe Johnston, Jessica Keating, Menna Khalil, Joseph Koerner, Jonathan Lear, Hugh Liebert, Mark Lilla, Bruce Lincoln, María Victoria Londoño-Becerra, Aditi Mody, Nathan Morello, Norma Moruzzi, David Moster, Mika Natif, Deborah Neibel, Kiersten Neumann, Alexander Orwin, James Osborne, Mathieu Ossendrijver, Davide Panagia, Robert Pippin, Jennifer Pitts, David Possen, Seth Richardson, Nathan Ristuccia, Francesca Rochberg, Larry Rothfield, Anna Seastrand, Michael Sells, George Shulman, Myron Silberstein, Daniel Silver, Laura Slatkin, Joel Snyder, Justin Steinberg, Irina Stelea, Richard Strier, Nathan Tarcov, Erin Thompson, Oya Topçuoğlu, Caroline Waerzeggers, Rosanna Warren, and Irene Winter. I'm particularly indebted to Susan Bielstein and James Whitman Toftnesss for their work on this book. The Neubauer Collegium for Culture and Society, the Division of the Humanities, and the Humanities Visiting Committee at the University of Chicago provided valuable research support.

NOTES

Prologue

1. Max Weber, "Politics as a Vocation," in *From Max Weber: Essays in Sociology*, ed. H. H. Gerth and C. Wright Mills (New York: Oxford University Press, 1946), 128.
2. Aristotle, *Politics*, trans. Ernest Barker (Oxford: Oxford University Press, 1995), II.5; translation modified by author.
3. *Dabiq* 7, February 12, 2015, 54–66.
4. Sherry Turkle, *Alone Together: Why We Expect More from Technology and Less from Each Other*, rev. and expanded ed. (New York: Basic Books, 2017), xxii.
5. Arnold Schoenberg, *Moses und Aron*, act II, scene 5.

Chapter 1

1. Sahih al-Bukhari 2478, in *Sahîh Al-Bukhari*, trans. Muhammad Muhsin Khan (Riyadh: Darussalam, 1997), 3:382.
2. Qur'anic quotations are from the translation by M. A. S. Abdel Haleem (Oxford: Oxford University Press, 2004), in some cases modified by author.
3. "Erasing the Legacy of a Ruined Nation," *Dabiq* 8, March 30, 2015, 22.
4. Al-Tabari, *The History of al-Ṭabarī*, vol. 2, *Prophets and Patriarchs*, trans. William M. Brinner (Albany: State University of New York Press, 1987), 50.
5. Al-Tabari, *History*, 2:61.
6. Alfarabi, *Philosophy of Plato and Aristotle*, rev. ed., trans. Muhsin Mahdi (Ithaca, NY: Cornell University Press, 2001), 23.
7. Alfarabi, *The Political Writings*, vol. 1, *"Selected Aphorisms" and Other Texts*, trans. Charles E. Butterworth (Ithaca, NY: Cornell University Press, 2001), 93.
8. Alfarabi, *Political Writings*, 1:95.

9. Alfarabi, *The Political Writings*, vol. 2, *"Political Regime" and "Summary of Plato's Law's,"* trans. Charles E. Butterworth (Ithaca, NY: Cornell University Press, 2015), 152–53; cf. Plato, *Laws*, 722c–723b.
10. Al-Tabari, *History*, 2:57–58.
11. Alfarabi, *Political Writings*, 2:75.
12. Alfarabi, *Political Writings*, 2:74.
13. Alfarabi, *Political Writings*, 2:74–75.
14. Alfarabi, *Political Writings*, 2:75.
15. Sahih Muslim 6:160–62. Quoted in Shahab Ahmed, *What Is Islam? The Importance of Being Islamic* (Princeton, NJ: Princeton University Press, 2016), p. 48.
16. Robyn Creswell and Bernard Haykel, "Battle Lines: Want to Understand the Jihadis? Read Their Poetry," *New Yorker*, June 1, 2015.
17. Quoted in William E. Shepard, "*Jāhiliyya*," in *The Princeton Encyclopedia of Islamic Political Thought*, ed. Gerhard Bowering (Princeton, NJ: Princeton University Press, 2013), 269.
18. Sayyid Qutb, *The Sayyid Qutb Reader: Selected Writings on Politics, Religion, and Society*, ed. Albert J. Bergesen (London: Routledge, 2008), 38.
19. Sayyid Qutb, *In the Shade of the Qur'an*, vol. 4, trans. Adil Salahi and Ashur Shamis (Leicester: Islamic Foundation, 2001), 133.
20. Raymond Geuss, *Politics and the Imagination* (Princeton, NJ: Princeton University Press, 2010), 115.
21. Carol Duncan, *Civilizing Rituals: Inside Public Art Museums* (London: Routledge, 1995), 8.

Chapter 2

1. Ann Marlowe, "Should Iraq's Archaeological Treasures Stay in the West?" *Daily Beast*, April 11, 2015, https://www.thedailybeast.com/should-iraqs-archaeological-treasures-stay-in-the-west.
2. "Iraq: UNESCO Outraged over Terrorist Attack against Mosul Museum," UN News, February 26, 2015, https://news.un.org/en/story/2015/02/492082-iraq-unesco-outraged-over-terrorist-attack-against-mosul-museum.
3. "UNESCO Director General Condemns Destruction of Nimrud in Iraq," UNESCO Media Services, March 6, 2015, http://www.unesco.org/

new/en/social-and-human-sciences/themes/human-rights-based-approach/sv3/news/unesco_director_general_condemns_destruction_of_nimrud_in_ir/.

4. "Statement by Thomas P. Campbell, director of the Metropolitan Museum of Art, on the Destruction at the Mosul Museum," February 26, 2015, https://www.metmuseum.org/press/news/2015/mosul-museum-destruction.
5. "Oriental Institute Statement on Cultural Destruction in Iraq," March 4, 2015, https://oi.uchicago.edu/about/statement-cultural-destruction-iraq.
6. "Statement on the Devastation of the Cultural Heritage of the Middle East," March 20, 2015, http://e-a-a.org/docs/EAA_statement.pdf.
7. "Azhar Slams ISIS for Bulldozing Nimrud," March 6, 2015, www.azhar.eg/observer-en/azhar-slams-isis-for-bulldozing-nimrud.
8. Hénri Grégoire, "Rapport sur les destructions opérées par le Vandalisme et les moyens de le réprimer (31 aout 1794)," http://www2.assemblee-nationale.fr/decouvrir-l-assemblee/histoire/grands-moments-d-eloquence/l-abbe-gregoire-31-aout-1794.
9. Quoted in Pierre Manent, *A World beyond Politics? A Defense of the Nation-State*, trans. Marc LePain (Princeton, NJ: Princeton University Press, 2006), 122.
10. Hannah Arendt, *The Promise of Politics* (New York: Schocken, 2005), 95.
11. Jules Mohl, *Lettres de M. Botta sur ses découvertes à Khorsabad près de Ninive* (Paris: Imprimerie Royale, 1844), 62.
12. Mohl, *Lettres de M. Botta*, 10.
13. Gustave Flaubert, *Voyage en Orient (1849–1851)*, ed. Claudine Gothot-Mersch (Paris: Gallimard, 2006), 248.
14. Austen Henry Layard, *Autobiography and Letters from His Childhood until His Appointment as H.M. Ambassador at Madrid*, ed. William N. Bruce (London: J. Murray, 1903), 311.
15. Quoted in Mogens Trolle Larsen, *The Conquest of Assyria: Excavations in an Antique Land* (London: Routledge, 1994), 70.
16. Quoted in Larsen, *Conquest of Assyria*, 99.
17. Quoted in Larsen, *Conquest of Assyria*, 132.
18. Mohl, *Lettres de M. Botta*, 26.
19. Quoted in Elisabeth Fontan, "Adrien de Longpérier et la création du

musée assyrien du Louvre," in *De Khorsabad à Paris: La découverte des Assyriens*, ed. Elisabeth Fontan (Paris: Réunion des Musées nationaux, 1994), 230.

20. Quoted in Larsen, *Conquest of Assyria*, 96.
21. Quoted in Lawrence Rothfield, *The Rape of Mesopotamia: Behind the Looting of the Iraq Museum* (Chicago: University of Chicago Press, 2009), 7.
22. Quoted in Edhem Eldem, "From Blissful Indifference to Anguished Concern: Ottoman Perceptions of Antiquities, 1799–1869," in *Scramble for the Past: A Story of Archaeology in the Ottoman Empire, 1753–1914*, ed. Zainab Bahrani, Zeynep Çelik, and Edhem Eldem (Istanbul: SALT, 2011), 320.
23. Quoted in John Malcolm Russell, *From Nineveh to New York: The Strange Story of the Assyrian Reliefs in the Metropolitan Museum and the Hidden Masterpiece at Canford School* (New Haven, CT: Yale University Press, 1997), 38.
24. Quoted in Frederick Bohrer, *Orientalism and Visual Culture: Imaging Mesopotamia in Nineteenth-Century Europe* (Cambridge: Cambridge University Press, 2003), 100.
25. Quoted in Sybil Gordon Kantor, *Alfred H. Barr, Jr., and the Intellectual Origins of the Museum of Modern Art* (Cambridge, MA: MIT Press, 2002), 318.
26. Henry Moore, *Writings and Conversations*, ed. Alan Wilkinson (Berkeley: University of California Press, 2002), 101.
27. Quoted in "The Tympanum within the Arch on the Doorway to the Oriental Institute: The Tympanum Explained," August 24, 2008, http://oihistory.blogspot.com/2008/08/tympanum-within-arch-on-doorway-to.html.
28. Austen Henry Layard, *Nineveh and Its Remains: A Narrative of an Expedition to Assyria* (London: J. Murray, 1867), 82.
29. "King Faysal's Coronation Speech, 1921," in *A Documentary History of Modern Iraq*, ed. Stacy E. Holden (Gainesville: University Press of Florida, 2012), 80.
30. Letter of Gertrude Bell to her father, Sir Hugh Bell, July 31, 1921, http://gertrudebell.ncl.ac.uk/letter_details.php?letter_id=495.

31. Quoted in Amatzia Baram, *Culture, History, and Ideology in the Formation of Ba'thist Iraq, 1968–89* (New York: St. Martin's, 1991), 27.
32. *Iraq: Travelling Art Exhibition* (Baghdad: National Gallery of Modern Art, 1965).
33. "Lorna Selim Remembers," in Maysaloun Faraj, *Strokes of Genius: Contemporary Iraqi Art* (London: Saqi Books, 2002), 43.
34. Baram, *Culture, History, and Ideology*, 28.
35. Quoted in Jabra I. Jabra, "The Crowning Achievement of Jewad Selim: The Monument of Liberty," *Gilgamesh: A Journal of Modern Iraqi Art* 1 (1987): 8.
36. Jabra, "Crowning Achievement," 9.
37. "The Ba'thist Constitution, 1970," in *Documentary History of Modern Iraq*, 196.
38. Quoted in Baram, *Culture, History, and Ideology*, 43.
39. Spencer Ackerman, "Toppled: How the Press Spun the 'Saddam Statue' Moment," *Wired*, January 3, 2011, https://www.wired.com/2011/01/toppled-how-the-press-spun-the-saddam-statue-moment/.
40. Fox News television coverage from April 9, 2003, https://www.youtube.com/watch?v=7TRVGlUMAik.
41. Sinan Antoon, *The Corpse Washer* (New Haven, CT: Yale University Press, 2013), 103.
42. "From Invisible Enemy to Enemy Kitchen: Michael Rakowitz in Conversation with Anthony Downey," *Ibraaz*, March 29, 2013, https://www.ibraaz.org/interviews/62.
43. Christiane Gruber, "Fighting ISIS with a Pen," *Newsweek*, June 26, 2015, https://www.newsweek.com/fighting-isis-pen-347335.

Chapter 3

1. Quoted in Mario Liverani, *Assyria: The Imperial Mission*, trans. Andrea Trameri and Jonathan Valk (Winona Lake, IN: Eisenbrauns, 2017), 73.
2. "British Jihadi Compares Syria War to *Call of Duty*," BBC Newsbeat, June 13, 2014, http://www.bbc.co.uk/newsbeat/article/27838978/british-jihadi-compares-syria-war-to-call-of-duty.
3. Johan Huizinga, *Homo Ludens: A Study of the Play-Element in Culture* (1938; London: Routledge & Kegan Paul, 1949), 28.

4. Huizinga, *Homo Ludens*, 206.
5. Wendy Brown, *Undoing the Demos: Neoliberalism's Stealth Revolution* (New York: Zone Books, 2015), 81.
6. Lev Grossman, "You—Yes, You—Are Time's Person of the Year," *Time*, December 25, 2006, http://content.time.com/time/magazine/article/0,9171,1570810,00.html.
7. "Facebook's Zuckerberg Wants to Figure Out Social Equation," http://www.terradaily.com/reports/Facebooks_Zuckerberg_wants_to_figure_out_social_equation_999.html.
8. Max Weber, *Economy and Society: An Outline of Interpretive Sociology*, ed. Guenther Roth and Claus Wittich (Berkeley: University of California Press, 1978), 973.
9. Jaron Lanier, *Who Owns the Future?* (New York: Simon & Schuster, 2014), 19.
10. David Kirkpatrick, *The Facebook Effect: The Inside Story of the Company That Is Connecting the Word* (New York: Simon and Schuster, 2010), 296.
11. "Everyone in Middle East Given Own Country in 317,000,000-State Solution," *Onion*, July 17, 2014, https://politics.theonion.com/everyone-in-middle-east-given-own-country-in-317-000-00-1819576713.
12. Hannah Arendt, *The Human Condition* (Chicago: University of Chicago Press, 1958), 160.
13. Quoted in Kara Swisher, "The Sum of Zuckerberg's Fears," *New York Times*, October 2, 2019.

Coda

1. Friedrich Nietzsche, *The Anti-Christ, Ecce Homo, Twilight of the Idols, and Other Writings*, ed. Aaron Ridley and Judith Norman (Cambridge: Cambridge University Press, 2005), 155.
2. Kynaston McShine, *The Museum as Muse: Artists Reflect* (New York: Museum of Modern Art, 1999), 116.
3. Plato, *Thaeatetus*, trans. Christopher Rowe (Cambridge: Cambridge University Press, 2015), 155d.
4. [Aristotle], *On Trolling*, trans. Rachel Barney, *Journal of the American Philosophical Association* 2 (2016): 194.

BIBLIOGRAPHY

Ahmed, Shahab. *What Is Islam? The Importance of Being Islamic*. Princeton, NJ: Princeton University Press, 2016.

Al-Bazzaz, ʿAbd al-Rahman. *On Arab Nationalism*. London: S. Austin, 1965.

Alfarabi. *On the Perfect State*. Revised text, with introduction and commentary by Richard Walzer. Oxford: Oxford University Press, 1985.

———. *Philosophy of Plato and Aristotle*. Translated by Muhsin Mahdi. Rev. ed. Ithaca, NY: Cornell University Press, 2001.

———. *The Political Writings*. Vol. 1, *"Selected Aphorisms" and Other Texts*. Translated by Charles E. Butterworth. Ithaca, NY: Cornell University Press, 2001.

———. *The Political Writings*. Vol. 2, *"Political Regime" and "Summary of Plato's Laws."* Translated by Charles E. Butterworth. Ithaca, NY: Cornell University Press, 2015.

Al-Tabari. *The History of al-Ṭabarī*. Vol. 2, *Prophets and Patriarchs*. Translated by William M. Brinner. Albany: State University of New York Press, 1987.

Antoon, Sinan. *The Corpse Washer*. New Haven, CT: Yale University Press, 2013.

Arendt, Hannah. *The Human Condition*. Chicago: University of Chicago Press, 1958.

———. *The Promise of Politics*. New York: Schocken, 2005.

———. *Responsibility and Judgment*. New York: Schocken, 2005.

Aristotle. *Politics*. Translated by Ernest Barker. Oxford: Oxford University Press, 1995.

[Aristotle]. *On Trolling*. Translated by Rachel Barney. *Journal of the American Philosophical Association* 2 (2016): 193–95.

Bahrani, Zainab. *The Infinite Image: Art, Time, and the Aesthetic Dimension in Antiquity*. London: Reaktion, 2014.

———. *Mesopotamia: Ancient Art and Architecture*. London: Thames & Hudson, 2017.

———. *Modernism and Iraq*. New York: Miriam and Ira D. Wallace Art Gallery, Columbia University, 2009.

Bahrani, Zainab, Zeynep Çelik, and Edhem Eldem, eds. *Scramble for the Past: A Story of Archaeology in the Ottoman Empire, 1753–1914*. Istanbul: SALT, 2011.

Baram, Amatzia. *Culture, History, and Ideology in the Formation of Ba'thist Iraq, 1968–89*. New York: St. Martin's, 1991.

Barnett, Richard D., Erika Bleibtreu, and Geoffrey Turner. *Sculptures from the Southwest Palace of Sennacherib at Nineveh*. 2 vols. London: British Museum Press, 1998.

Bell, Gertrude. *A Woman in Arabia: The Writings of the Queen of the Desert*. Edited by Georgina Howell. New York: Penguin, 2015.

Bernhardsson, Magnus T. *Reclaiming a Plundered Past: Archaeology and Nation Building in Modern Iraq*. Austin: University of Texas Press, 2005.

Bohrer, Frederick. *Orientalism and Visual Culture: Imaging Mesopotamia in Nineteenth-Century Europe*. Cambridge: Cambridge University Press, 2003.

Brown, Wendy. *Undoing the Demos: Neoliberalism's Stealth Revolution*. New York: Zone Books, 2015.

Brusasco, Paolo. "The Assyrian Sculptures in the Mosul Cultural Museum: A Preliminary Assessment of What Was on Display before Islamic State's Attack." *Journal of Near Eastern Studies* 75 (2016): 205–48.

Duncan, Carol. *Civilizing Rituals: Inside Public Art Museums*. London: Routledge, 1995.

Flood, Finbarr Barry. "Between Cult and Culture: Bamiyan, Islamic Iconoclasm and the Museum." *Art Bulletin* 84 (2002): 641–59.

———. "Idol Breaking as Image Making in the 'Islamic State.'" *Religion and Society: Advances in Research* 7 (2016): 116–38.

Galloway, Alexander R. *Gaming: Essays on Algorithmic Culture*. Minneapolis: University of Minnesota Press, 2006.

Gamboni, Dario. *The Destruction of Art: Iconoclasm and Vandalism since the French Revolution*. London: Reaktion, 1997.

Goldziher, Ignaz. *Introduction to Islamic Theology*. Translated by Andras and Ruth Hamori. Princeton, NJ: Princeton University Press, 1981.

Harmanşah, Ömür. "ISIS, Heritage, and the Spectacles of Destruction in the Global Media." *Near Eastern Archaeology* 78 (2015): 170–77.

Hebrew Bible, The. Translation and commentary by Robert Alter. 3 vols. New York: W. W. Norton, 2019.

Hobbes, Thomas. *Leviathan*. Edited by Edwin Curley. Indianapolis: Hackett, 1994.

Huizinga, Johan. *Homo Ludens: A Study of the Play Element in Culture*. 1938; London: Routledge & Kegan Paul, 1949.

Huxley, Julian. *UNESCO: Its Purpose and Its Philosophy*. Washington: Public Affairs Press, 1947.

Jabra, Jabra I. "The Crowning Achievement of Jewad Selim: The Monument of Liberty." *Gilgamesh: A Journal of Modern Iraqi Art* 1 (1987): 7–11.

Kantor, Sybil Gordon. *Alfred H. Barr, Jr., and the Intellectual Origins of the Museum of Modern Art*. Cambridge, MA: MIT Press, 2002.

Lanier, Jaron. *Who Owns the Future?* New York: Simon & Schuster, 2014.

———. *You Are Not a Gadget: A Manifesto*. New York: Vintage, 2010.

Larsen, Mogens Trolle. *The Conquest of Assyria: Excavations in an Antique Land*. London: Routledge, 1994.

Latour, Bruno. "A Few Steps towards the Anthropology of the Iconoclastic Gesture." *Science in Context* 10 (1998): 63–83.

Layard, Austen Henry. *Nineveh and Its Remains*. London: J. Murray, 1849.

Liverani, Mario. *Assyria: The Imperial Mission*. Translated by Andrea Trameri and Jonathan Valk. Winona Lake, IN: Eisenbrauns, 2017.

Manent, Pierre. *A World beyond Politics? A Defense of the Nation-State*. Translated by Marc LePain. Princeton, NJ: Princeton University Press, 2006.

McClellan, Andrew. *Inventing the Louvre: Art, Politics, and the Origins of the Modern Museum in Eighteenth-Century Paris*. Cambridge: Cambridge University Press, 1994.

Melville, Sarah C. *The Campaigns of Sargon II, King of Assyria, 721–705 B.C.* Norman: University of Oklahoma Press, 2016.

Moore, Henry. *Writings and Conversations*. Edited by Alan Wilkinson. Berkeley: University of California Press, 2002.

Nietzsche, Friedrich. *The Anti-Christ, Ecce Homo, Twilight of the Idols, and Other Writings*. Edited by Aaron Ridley and Judith Norman. Cambridge: Cambridge University Press, 2005.

Plato. *Theaetetus and Sophist*. Edited and translated by Christopher Rowe. Cambridge: Cambridge University Press, 2015.

Qur'an. Translated by M. A. S. Abdel Haleem. Oxford: Oxford University Press, 2004.

Qutb, Sayyid. *In the Shade of the Qur'an*. Vol. 4. Translated by Adil Salahi and Ashur Shamis. Leicester: Islamic Foundation, 2001.

———. *The Sayyid Qutb Reader: Selected Writings on Politics, Religion, and Society*. Edited by Albert J. Bergesen. London: Routledge, 2008.

Radner, Karen. "Economy, Society, and Daily Life in the Neo-Assyrian Period." In *A Companion to Assyria*, edited by Eckart Frahm, 209–28. Malden, MA: Wiley Blackwell, 2007.

Robson, Eleanor. *Mathematics in Ancient Iraq: A Social History*. Princeton, NJ: Princeton University Press, 2008.

Russell, John Malcolm. "Bulls for the Palace and Order in the Empire: The Sculptural Program of Sennacherib's Court VI at Nineveh." *Art Bulletin* 69 (1987): 520–39.

———. *From Nineveh to New York: The Strange Story of the Assyrian Reliefs in the Metropolitan Museum and the Hidden Masterpiece at Canford School*. New Haven, CT: Yale University Press, 1997.

Shaw, Wendy M. K. *Possessors and Possessed: Museums, Archaeology, and the Visualization of History in the Late Ottoman Empire*. Berkeley: University of California Press, 2003.

Simanowski, Roberto. *Facebook Society: Losing Ourselves in Sharing Ourselves*. Translated by Susan H. Gillespie. New York: Columbia University Press, 2018.

Somekh, Sasson. *Baghdad, Yesterday: The Making of an Arab Jew*. Jerusalem: Ibis Editions, 2007.

Stern, Jessica, and J. M. Berger. *ISIS: The State of Terror*. New York: Ecco, 2016.

Turkle, Sherry. *Alone Together: Why We Expect More from Technology and Less from Each Other*. Revised and Expanded Edition. New York: Basic Books, 2017.

Ursinus, Michael. "The Ruins of Dura-Europos in the Columns of Zevra: Ahmed Sakir Beg's Travels along the Euphrates, Published and Annotated by the Provincial Gazette of Baghdad." In *Middle Eastern Press as a Forum of Literature*, edited by Horst Unbehaun, 167–80. Frankfurt am Main: Verlag Peter Lang, 2004.

van Dijck, José. *The Culture of Connectivity: A Critical History of Social Media*. Oxford: Oxford University Press, 2013.

Visser, Reidar. "Proto-Political Conceptions of 'Iraq' in Late Ottoman Times." *International Journal of Contemporary Iraqi Studies* 3 (2009): 143–54.

Voorhees, Gerald A., Josh Call, and Katie Whitlock, eds. *Guns, Grenades, and Grunts: First-Person Shooter Games*. London: Bloomsbury, 2012.

Weber, Max. *Economy and Society: An Outline of Interpretive Sociology*. Edited by Guenther Roth and Claus Wittich. Berkeley: University of California Press, 1978.

———. *From Max Weber: Essays in Sociology*. Edited by H. H. Gerth and C. Wright Mills. Oxford: Oxford University Press, 1946.

Winter, Irene. *On Art in the Ancient Near East*. 2 vols. Leiden: Brill, 2009.

www.ingramcontent.com/pod-product-compliance
Lightning Source LLC
LaVergne TN
LVHW010625100826
845148LV00014B/3116